PERFORMANCE MANAGEMENT

EXCELLENCE IN ORGANIZATIONAL PERFORMANCE

DR. VIDHYA K.

To all the dedicated managers and employees striving to improve their performance and achieve their goals through effective performance management. Your commitment to excellence inspires us all.

Contents

Foreword

Performance management is critical to the success of any organization, large or small. Effective performance management ensures that the right people are in the right roles, with the right skills and knowledge to achieve their goals. It also ensures that employees are motivated, engaged, and committed to the organization's mission and values.

This book on performance management is a valuable resource for managers, HR professionals, and anyone interested in improving organizational performance. The book provides practical guidance on how to design and implement effective performance management processes, including goal setting, performance feedback, coaching, and development.

The authors draw on their extensive experience in performance management and provide practical insights and real-life examples to illustrate their points. They also highlight the importance of aligning performance management with the organization's strategy and culture, and the need for ongoing monitoring and evaluation.

As someone who has been involved in performance management for many years, I highly recommend this book to anyone seeking to improve their organization's performance. It is a valuable resource for both novice and experienced practitioners, and I am confident that it will help you achieve your performance management goals.

Sincerely,

Preface

Performance management is an essential component of any organization's success. However, it can be a complex and challenging process to design and implement. This book aims to provide practical guidance and insights into performance management to help organizations achieve their goals and objectives.

The book is structured to take readers through the various stages of performance management, starting with goal-setting and planning, followed by performance monitoring and feedback, coaching and development, and finally, evaluating performance and making necessary improvements.

We draw on our collective experience in performance management, as well as insights from leading experts in the field, to provide practical advice and real-life examples to illustrate key concepts. We also address common challenges and pitfalls that organizations may encounter and provide suggestions for overcoming them.

The book is intended for managers, HR professionals, and anyone interested in improving organizational performance through effective performance management. We hope that this book will serve as a valuable resource to help organizations develop and implement effective performance management processes that enable their employees to achieve their full potential.

Sincerely,

[Dr. VIDHYA K.]

Enter Caption

CHAPTER ONE

Performance Management – an Introduction

Objectives

We will be able to accomplish the following after studying this unit:

• A description of how performance management works and its characteristics

• Outline the performance management objectives and principles

• Analyze the performance appraisal and performance management process

• Describe the challenges faced by performance management

Introduction

An organization's power is increasingly determined by its intellectual capital, rather than by its physical assets. Competitiveness and performance of corporations are largely driven by people. The purpose of performance management is to improve the performance of employees in order to improve organizational performance. Costs associated with competitiveness are money and productivity. Approximately 60 percent of the total cost of an organization can be attributed to workforce productivity, according to Dr Mritunjay Arthreya (2004). Consequently, performance management's growing significance does not need to be explained further.

1.1 Concept of Performance

A company's survival depends on its ability to compete. Survival for the fittest is exactly what it sounds like. Performance is the only way to achieve this. There is no point in settling for ordinary performance. Despite better performance, it may not be sufficient. Competing and thriving requires the company to perform at its best.

Performance Defined

As defined by the Oxford English Dictionary, 'performance' as behaviour—the way in which organizations, teams and individuals get work done.

According to Campbell (1990), "Performance is behaviour that should be distinguished from outcomes since they may be affected by system factors".

A more comprehensive view of performance can be achieved if it encompasses both behaviour and outcomes.

As Brumbrach (1988) says: "Performance means both behaviours and results. Behaviours emanate from the performer and transform performance from abstraction to action. Not just instruments for results, behaviours are also outcomes in their own right—the product or mental and physical effort applied to tasks—and can be judged apart from results."

Performance could, therefore, be considered behaviour—the way in which organizations, teams and individuals get work done. Campbell believes that 'Performance is behaviour and should be distinguished from outcomes because they can be contaminated by systems factors.'

A performance is a play, concert, or other form of entertainment. Furthermore, it can be defined as the act or process of carrying out or accomplishing something.

In simple terms, Performance = skill + will

To create skill: It means to ensure that we have the resources and infrastructure to perform. They are mainly:

1) Machine

2) Money

3) Material

4) the workforce.

They determine an organization's capacity.

It is impossible to achieve better performance without state-of-the-art machinery that is superior or equal to that of competitors.

Performance will be hampered by a lack of money or inadequate materials. The strategic availability of these resources is therefore essential.

The workforce is a critical and scarce resource, as well as a strategic one. A successful organization sources, attracts, develops, retains, and motivates talent.

The Pillars of Human Performance

There are three dimensions in which an individual's work performance may be observed and appraised:

1. Understanding the context of work, or the work situation, in terms of its purpose, nature, conditions, requirements, appraisal metrics, etc.
2. The ability to perform work effectively in terms of the knowledge, skills, and capabilities associated with performance excellence; and
3. An exceptional commitment to performing the work and putting forth best efforts.

Understanding the context, effectiveness, and motivation to excel may be seen as three pillars of human performance. The three axes of human performance can be logically applied and instantiated to explain the nature, norms, and attributes of human capital as follows:

The first pillar of the framework, i.e., understanding the context, requires employees to reflect and critically examine the dynamic business environment of their enterprises. Additionally, they should be familiar with their company's vision and strategy, business model and profit model, competitive logic, and core value proposition. This requires employees to have a clear understanding of the company's processes, mechanisms, and methods of creating, capturing, and delivering value. Likewise, it implies their own individual and collective efforts to realize their company's vision and strategy. Employees with a better understanding of their company's business context are also better able to recognize the current and potential challenges their company faces, as well as the necessary knowledge, skills, and capabilities to cope with them.

The second pillar of human capital is the ability to be effective, which implies employees' dedication to work excellence in their broadly defined and non-rigid work roles. Further, it implies employees' sustained commitment to learning, upgrading skills, developing new and necessary capabilities, expertise, creative thinking and using knowledge; both for problem-solving and innovation; streamlining processes, procedures, and routines to eliminate non-value-adding activities; and experimenting and taking initiative to find new opportunities. Excellence in performance, or effectiveness, does not remain static or fixed over time.

The second pillar of human capital is significantly shaped by the first (understanding the business context) in terms of adaptability to changing business environments. Organizational and industry life cycles, as well as employee learning, knowledge, skills, and capabilities. Organizations ranging from high-tech growth firms to mature or declining industries, or firms caught up in industrial shake-outs and consolidations, would perform dramatically differently. The requirements of a firm may vary from time to time based on changes in its competitive environment. In the second axis of performance, human capital is focused on proactive learning, development, and application of knowledge to deliver outstanding work for customers.

In the third pillar, "motivation for excellence", employees are encouraged to work together to achieve the enterprise's goals, as well as expressing a strong commitment to them. Consequently, they imply a high degree of trust and goodwill among employees. To solve difficult problems creatively, individuals who possess complementary and specialized skills and knowledge need to collaborate with commitment and cooperation. Developing new products and/or services, achieving performance breakthroughs, creating new competencies, and continuously improving and innovating are all part of this process.

An enterprise's employees must score high on each of the three axes, both individually and collectively. A firm's human capital must score consistently across all three axes and expand over time. There is a fundamental question regarding how the performance requirements above can be met continuously. How do you scale up to performance heights, and maintain that level of performance in a sustainable manner?

Apart from an individual's ability and motivation, performance excellence and effectiveness in organizations are largely determined by how effectively an individual collaborates with others. Collaborating is about trust, mutual respect, sharing ideas, information, knowledge, and resources. Ultimately, it is about working together to learn, solve problems, innovate, meet tight deadlines, cope with obstacles, deal with unforeseen difficulties, and strive to achieve and exceed organizational goals. There may be a variety of collaborative activities and collaborating individuals, a variety of team members, and new forms of interpersonal and group interaction may result from rotating job assignments across organizational levels, space, and time when the collaborating persons or team members. The imperatives of doing one's best in cooperation with others, helping others when needed, and pursuing the stretch goals of the enterprise remain the same.

The Performance Management Cycle

An organization's performance management is a process, which is not a spontaneous event. The process operates as a continuous cycle, as illustrated in Figure 1.1

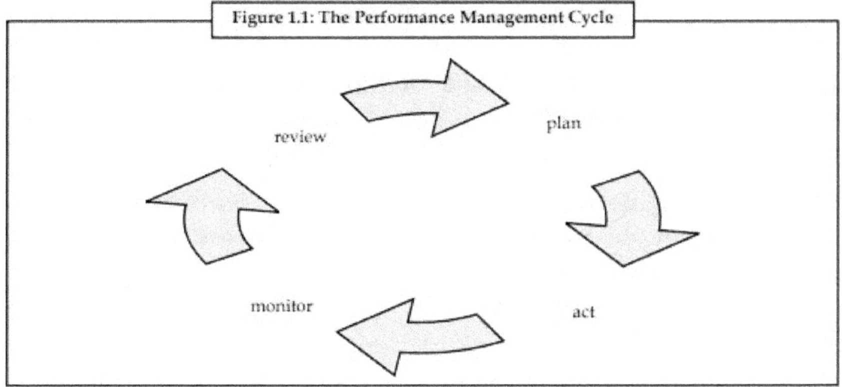

Enter Caption

1.2 Concept of Performance Management

A performance management concept can be divided into two types. The first evaluates an organization's performance as a whole and its managers' effectiveness. Second, the organization must evaluate its employees to ensure they achieve reasonable goals in order to perform better.

Enter Caption

It is essential to understand performance. The performer's behaviour transforms performance from abstraction to action. A behaviour is not just an instrument for results, but also an outcome in itself. It is the product of mental and physical effort applied to a task, and it is distinct from the outcome. Organizational performance refers to the successful formulation and implementation of value-creating strategies that support the organization's competitiveness.

A Successful Performance Management Plan Must Include the Following Ingredients
• Dedicated leadership
• Performance transparency
• Establish a competency-based development plan
• A multi-source feedback mechanism that is effective in discussing and addressing performance issues
• Program results are strongly correlated with performance measures
• Measuring performance usefully

Consequently, performance management helps organizations manage consistent performance in a manner that holds employees and managers accountable for supporting its objectives and strategy, successfully fulfilling assigned job responsibilities, and accomplishing individual performance goals. As a prerequisite, the following would be required:

1) Processes are as simple as possible
2) Leadership and management are clearly defined
3) Empowering employees leads to innovation
4) Having a distinct organizational culture
5) In the workplace, honesty, integrity, and trust are essential
6) An openness to change

Overview of performance management

Performance management is the process of setting goals, measuring progress, providing feedback, and taking corrective action to improve individual, team, and organizational performance. It involves creating a culture of continuous improvement and aligning employee performance with organizational goals and strategies. The key components of performance management include setting clear expectations, providing feedback and coaching, evaluating performance, and rewarding or addressing performance gaps. The goals of performance management include improving employee productivity, enhancing employee engagement and motivation, fostering employee development, and ensuring the achievement of organizational objectives. Effective performance management requires a commitment from leadership, clear communication, and ongoing training and support for employees.

Importance of performance management

Performance management is essential for organizations to achieve their goals, improve productivity, and maintain a competitive edge in the market. Here are some of the key reasons why performance management is important:

• Goal alignment: Performance management helps to align employee goals with the organization's objectives, ensuring that everyone is working towards the same vision and mission.

• Improved communication: Performance management facilitates ongoing communication between employees and their managers, allowing for regular feedback, coaching, and support.

• Enhanced productivity: By setting clear expectations and providing feedback and support, performance management can improve employee productivity, leading to increased efficiency and effectiveness.

• Employee development: Performance management provides opportunities for employee development, allowing employees to grow and develop their skills and knowledge.

• Employee engagement: Performance management can increase employee engagement by providing a sense of purpose, motivation, and recognition for their efforts.

• Retention of top talent: Effective performance management can help to retain top talent by providing clear career paths, growth opportunities, and recognition for their contributions.

• Legal compliance: Performance management can help organizations ensure compliance with legal requirements, such as equal employment opportunity laws and performance-based pay regulations.

In summary, performance management is critical for organizations to achieve their goals, improve productivity, retain top talent, and maintain legal compliance.

The key components of performance management

• Goal setting: Setting clear, specific, and measurable goals is a crucial component of performance management. Goals should be aligned with the organization's objectives and strategies, and should be set in collaboration between employees and their managers.

• Performance monitoring: Regular monitoring of performance helps managers track progress towards goals, identify areas for improvement, and provide feedback and support to employees.

• Feedback and coaching: Providing regular feedback and coaching is essential for employee development and performance improvement. Feedback should be specific, timely, and focused on behaviors and outcomes, rather than personal characteristics.

• Performance evaluation: Evaluating performance is a key component of performance management, allowing managers to assess employee performance against established goals and objectives. Performance evaluations should be fair, objective, and based on established criteria.

• Performance improvement: Addressing performance gaps is an essential component of performance management. Managers should work with employees to identify areas for improvement, develop improvement plans, and provide support and resources as needed.

• Reward and recognition: Providing rewards and recognition is an essential component of performance management, motivating and engaging employees to achieve their goals and objectives. Rewards can include monetary incentives, promotions, or non-monetary rewards such as public recognition or increased autonomy.

By implementing these key components, organizations can establish a culture of continuous improvement and ensure that employee performance is aligned with organizational goals and strategies.

The different types of performance management systems

There are several types of performance management systems that organizations can implement, including:

• Traditional performance management systems: These systems are typically based on annual or semi-annual reviews, where managers rate employee performance against predetermined goals and competencies.

• Continuous performance management systems: These systems focus on ongoing feedback and coaching, rather than formal annual or semi-annual reviews. They emphasize regular check-ins between employees and managers to discuss progress towards goals and provide feedback and support.

• 360-degree feedback systems: These systems involve gathering feedback from a range of sources, including managers, peers, subordinates, and even external stakeholders, to provide a more comprehensive view of an employee's performance.

• Objective-based performance management systems: These systems focus on setting and achieving specific objectives, rather than relying on subjective ratings or assessments. They emphasize clear and measurable goals, ongoing feedback, and regular check-ins to monitor progress towards objectives.

• Results-based performance management systems: These systems focus on measuring and rewarding outcomes, rather than inputs or activities. They emphasize setting clear performance targets and measuring results against those targets.

• Competency-based performance management systems: These systems focus on assessing and developing specific competencies or skills that are critical to job performance. They emphasize ongoing feedback and coaching to develop and improve these competencies.

By understanding the different types of performance management systems, organizations can choose the approach that best aligns with their goals and strategies, and that will be most effective in improving employee performance and driving organizational success.

The goals of performance management
The goals of performance management are to:

1) Improve employee productivity: Performance management aims to improve employee productivity by providing clear expectations, feedback, coaching, and support. This can lead to increased efficiency, effectiveness, and output.

2) Enhance employee engagement and motivation: Performance management aims to enhance employee engagement and motivation by providing a sense of purpose, recognition, and career development opportunities. This can lead to increased job satisfaction, commitment, and loyalty.

3) Foster employee development: Performance management aims to foster employee development by providing opportunities for learning, growth, and skill development. This can lead to increased employee competence, confidence, and career advancement.

4) Align individual performance with organizational goals and strategies: Performance management aims to align individual performance with organizational goals and strategies, ensuring that everyone is working

towards the same vision and mission. This can lead to increased organizational effectiveness and success.

5) Ensure the achievement of organizational objectives: Performance management aims to ensure the achievement of organizational objectives by setting clear performance expectations, monitoring progress, and taking corrective action as needed. This can lead to increased organizational performance and success.

Overall, the goals of performance management are to create a culture of continuous improvement, align employee performance with organizational goals, and drive employee and organizational success. By achieving these goals, organizations can improve productivity, engagement, and overall effectiveness.

The steps involved in implementing an effective performance management system

Implementing an effective performance management system involves several key steps, including:

1) Define performance expectations: Clearly define performance expectations for each role and individual, aligning them with organizational goals and strategies. These expectations should be specific, measurable, achievable, relevant, and time-bound (SMART).

2) Establish a performance management process: Develop a performance management process that includes goal setting, ongoing feedback, coaching, evaluation, and reward and recognition.

3) Train managers and employees: Train managers and employees on the performance management process, providing guidance on how to set goals, provide feedback, evaluate performance, and provide reward and recognition.

4) Communicate expectations and process: Communicate performance expectations and the performance management process to all employees, ensuring that they understand what is expected of them and how they will be evaluated.

5) Monitor and evaluate performance: Regularly monitor and evaluate employee performance against established goals and expectations. Provide ongoing feedback and coaching to help employees improve performance and reach their goals.

6) Provide recognition and rewards: Provide recognition and rewards to employees who achieve their goals and exceed expectations, motivating them to continue to perform at a high level.

7) Review and improve the process: Regularly review and improve the performance management process, incorporating feedback from managers and employees, and making adjustments as needed to ensure that it remains effective and relevant.

By following these steps, organizations can implement an effective performance management system that aligns individual and organizational goals, drives employee development and engagement, and improves overall organizational performance.

1.3 Characteristics of Performance Management

Performance management has the following key characteristics:

1. Performance management is a crucial organizational tool to clarify performance objectives, standards, critical dimensions, and competencies to enhance individual performance.

2. Performance management works best when employee work is planned and achievement goals are communicated.

3. It emphasizes the development of the capability and capacity of employees to perform consistently, coupled with the agility to respond to a changing dynamic business and work environment.

4. Performance management is a 'systematic' and 'holistic' approach to identifying critical dimensions of performance.

5. It helps in integrating the performance management process with other critical organizational systems including leadership development, succession planning, and talent management efforts.

6. Performance management is a multidimensional concept and includes inputs, processes, outputs and outcomes.

7. Performance management transforms organizational objectives and strategy into a measurable action plan. This is done by getting the right information to and from the right people at the right time and in the right format.

1.4 Objectives of Performance Management

The objectives of performance management are as follows:

1) Improve employee performance: Performance management aims to improve employee performance by setting clear expectations, providing feedback, and identifying opportunities for improvement. This can lead to increased productivity, efficiency, and effectiveness.

2) Develop employee skills and competencies: Performance management aims to develop employee skills and competencies by

providing training, coaching, and career development opportunities. This can lead to increased employee engagement, satisfaction, and retention.

3) Align employee performance with organizational goals: Performance management aims to align employee performance with organizational goals and strategies, ensuring that everyone is working towards the same vision and mission. This can lead to increased organizational effectiveness and success.

4) Identify high performers and potential leaders: Performance management aims to identify high-performing employees and potential future leaders, providing opportunities for advancement and career growth. This can lead to increased employee motivation and loyalty, as well as increased organizational performance.

5) Foster a culture of continuous improvement: Performance management aims to foster a culture of continuous improvement by encouraging ongoing feedback, learning, and development. This can lead to increased innovation, adaptability, and agility, which are critical for organizational success in today's rapidly changing business environment.

Overall, the objectives of performance management are to improve employee and organizational performance, develop employee skills and competencies, align individual and organizational goals, and foster a culture of continuous improvement. By achieving these objectives, organizations can drive employee and organizational success, and achieve their strategic objectives.

1.5 Principles of Performance Management
The principles of performance management are:

1) Alignment: Performance management should align individual performance with organizational goals and strategies. This requires clearly defining performance expectations and communicating how individual performance contributes to the achievement of organizational objectives.

2) Clarity: Performance management should be clear and transparent, with clear performance expectations, feedback, and evaluation criteria. This helps employees understand what is expected of them and how they will be evaluated.

3) Continuous improvement: Performance management should foster a culture of continuous improvement, with ongoing feedback, coaching, and development opportunities. This helps employees develop their skills and competencies, and ensures that the organization remains agile and adaptable in a rapidly changing business environment.

4) Fairness: Performance management should be fair and unbiased, with objective evaluation criteria and equal opportunities for all employees. This helps build trust and engagement among employees, and ensures that high-performing employees are recognized and rewarded appropriately.

5) Participation: Performance management should involve active participation from both managers and employees. This requires regular feedback and coaching from managers, as well as active engagement from employees in setting goals and evaluating their own performance.

6) Accountability: Performance management should be accountable, with clear expectations and consequences for both high and low performance. This helps ensure that employees are responsible for their own performance, and that the organization achieves its strategic objectives.

Overall, the principles of performance management are to align individual and organizational goals, provide clarity and transparency, foster continuous improvement, ensure fairness and participation, and promote accountability. By following these principles, organizations can create a culture of high performance, engagement, and success.

Top Ten Performance Management Tips

Here are ten top performance management tips:

1) Set clear and measurable goals: Ensure that performance goals are specific, measurable, achievable, relevant, and time-bound (SMART).

2) Provide ongoing feedback: Regularly provide feedback to employees on their performance, focusing on strengths, weaknesses, and opportunities for improvement.

3) Encourage employee self-evaluation: Encourage employees to evaluate their own performance, setting goals and identifying areas for improvement.

4) Use data and analytics: Use data and analytics to track and evaluate performance, identifying trends and areas for improvement.

5) Recognize and reward high performance: Recognize and reward high-performing employees, providing incentives and recognition to motivate and engage them.

6) Provide development opportunities: Provide development opportunities to help employees develop their skills and competencies, improving their performance and engagement.

7) Create a culture of continuous improvement: Foster a culture of continuous improvement, encouraging ongoing learning, innovation, and

adaptation.

8) Train managers on effective performance management: Train managers on effective performance management techniques, including how to provide feedback, evaluate performance, and provide coaching and development opportunities.

9) Conduct regular performance reviews: Conduct regular performance reviews, providing opportunities for employees to discuss their performance, ask questions, and provide feedback.

10) Communicate performance expectations: Communicate performance expectations clearly and regularly, ensuring that employees understand what is expected of them and how they will be evaluated.

By following these top performance management tips, organizations can improve employee engagement, productivity, and overall organizational performance.

1.6 Performance Appraisal to Performance Management

Performance appraisal is a part of performance management, but it is not the same thing. Performance appraisal is a process of evaluating employee performance at a given point in time, usually annually. It involves reviewing employee performance against pre-defined goals and objectives, and providing feedback on strengths, weaknesses, and areas for improvement. Performance appraisal typically results in a performance rating or score, which is used to inform decisions about promotions, salary increases, or other rewards.

Performance management, on the other hand, is a more comprehensive and ongoing process that involves setting performance expectations, providing feedback and coaching, and supporting employee development and growth. It is focused on improving employee performance and aligning individual performance with organizational goals and strategies. Performance management includes a range of activities such as goal setting, ongoing feedback and coaching, development planning, and performance evaluation. It is a continuous process that takes place throughout the year, rather than a once-a-year event.

While performance appraisal is a part of performance management, it is just one component of a broader approach to managing employee performance. Performance management focuses on ongoing communication and development, rather than just a once-a-year evaluation. By shifting from performance appraisal to performance management, organizations can create a culture of continuous improvement and support employee development and growth, which can lead to improved engagement, productivity, and organizational success.

Performance Appraisal vs. Performance Management

Performance appraisal and performance management are related but distinct concepts in the realm of managing employee performance.

Performance appraisal is a formal process in which an employee's job performance is evaluated and assessed based on pre-defined criteria. It typically involves a supervisor or manager providing feedback on an employee's work over a specific time period, such as a year or six months. The results of the appraisal can be used to determine an employee's strengths and weaknesses, identify areas for improvement, and make decisions regarding promotion, compensation, or termination.

Performance management, on the other hand, is a broader and ongoing process of managing employee performance that focuses on achieving organizational goals and objectives. It includes a range of activities, such as goal setting, regular feedback and coaching, development planning, and performance evaluation. Performance management is focused on continuous improvement, and it involves ongoing communication between managers and employees to ensure that everyone is aligned and working towards the same goals.

While performance appraisal is typically a once-a-year event, performance management is an ongoing process that takes place throughout the year. Performance appraisal is just one aspect of performance management, and it is often used as a tool to support the broader performance management process.

In summary, performance appraisal is a tool used within the performance management process to assess employee performance, whereas performance management is a broader process of managing and improving employee performance over time.

Performance Appraisal	Performance Management
Focus is on top-down assessment	Stresses on mutual objective setting through a process of joint dialogue
Performed annually	Continuous reviews are performed
Usage of ratings is very common	Usage of ratings is less common
Focus is on traits	Focus is on quantifiable objectives, values and behaviours
Monolithic system	Flexible system
Are very much linked with pay	Is not directly linked with pay

Enter Caption

1.7 Challenges to Performance Management

While performance management can be a valuable tool for managing employee performance and improving organizational outcomes, there are several challenges that organizations may face when implementing a performance management system. Some common challenges include:

1) Resistance to change: Employees may be resistant to changes in performance management practices, particularly if they are used to a traditional, top-down approach to evaluation and feedback.

2) Limited resources: Implementing an effective performance management system requires time, resources, and expertise. Organizations may face challenges in allocating the necessary resources to create a robust performance management process.

3) Lack of training: Managers may lack the necessary training or experience to provide effective feedback and coaching, which can limit the effectiveness of the performance management process.

4) Inconsistent application: If the performance management process is not applied consistently across the organization, it can lead to inequities and perceptions of bias.

5) Unrealistic expectations: Setting unrealistic goals or expectations can lead to employee burnout and disengagement, which can undermine the effectiveness of the performance management process.

6) Lack of alignment: If individual performance goals and objectives are not aligned with organizational goals and objectives, it can lead to a lack of focus and coordination.

7) Evaluation bias: Performance evaluation can be subject to bias, particularly if evaluators are not trained on how to provide objective and unbiased feedback.

8) Inadequate technology: Lack of technology or outdated technology can limit the effectiveness of the performance management process, particularly when it comes to tracking and analyzing performance data.

By being aware of these challenges, organizations can take steps to address them and improve the effectiveness of their performance management process. This may include investing in training and development for managers, ensuring consistent application of the process, setting realistic goals and expectations, and using technology to support the process.

 Identify the key challenges faced by Indian companies in the area of HR

Enter Caption

Top ten Performance Management case studies

Here are ten case studies that showcase successful examples of performance management:

1) Deloitte: Deloitte revamped its performance management process by eliminating traditional performance ratings and shifting towards continuous feedback and coaching approach. This change led to increased employee engagement and productivity.

2) General Electric: General Electric implemented a "rank and yank" system, in which employees were ranked and the bottom performers were fired. While controversial, this approach led to a culture of high performance and accountability.

3) Google: Google uses a performance management system that includes regular check-ins, goal setting, and peer feedback. This approach has been credited with contributing to the company's success in innovation and employee satisfaction.

4) Infosys: Infosys implemented a performance management system that includes a 360-degree feedback process, ongoing training and development, and regular performance evaluations. This system has helped the company

achieve high levels of employee engagement and retention.

5) Intel: Intel implemented a system that measures employee performance based on the completion of specific tasks, rather than subjective evaluations. This approach has led to improved employee performance and greater transparency in the performance management process.

6) Procter & Gamble: Procter & Gamble uses a performance management system that includes regular check-ins, coaching and feedback, and individual development plans. This approach has helped the company achieve high levels of employee engagement and retention.

7) Southwest Airlines: Southwest Airlines uses a performance management system that focuses on core values, teamwork, and customer service. This approach has helped the company achieve high levels of customer satisfaction and employee engagement.

8) Tata Consultancy Services: Tata Consultancy Services uses a performance management system that includes regular feedback, goal setting, and individual development plans. This system has helped the company achieve high levels of employee engagement and retention.

9) Toyota: Toyota uses a performance management system that includes regular performance evaluations, coaching and feedback, and individual development plans. This approach has helped the company achieve high levels of employee engagement and continuous improvement.

10) Zappos: Zappos uses a performance management system that includes regular check-ins, coaching and feedback, and individual development plans. This approach has helped the company achieve high levels of employee engagement and customer satisfaction.

These case studies demonstrate the effectiveness of a variety of performance management approaches, from continuous feedback to goal setting to peer evaluations. By tailoring their performance management systems to the specific needs and goals of their organizations, companies can achieve higher levels of employee engagement, productivity, and organizational success.

Performance Management in Tata Iron and Steel Company (TISCO)

Tata Iron and Steel Company (TISCO), now known as Tata Steel, is one of the largest steel manufacturers in India. The company has a long history of implementing innovative performance management practices to improve the performance of its employees and achieve its business goals.

TISCO's performance management system is based on a combination of individual performance, team performance, and organizational performance. The system is designed to be transparent, objective, and results-oriented, and it includes several key elements:

1) Performance planning: At the beginning of each year, managers and employees work together to set individual and team goals that are aligned with the company's strategic objectives. These goals are based on the SMART criteria (specific, measurable, achievable, relevant, and time-bound) to ensure they are meaningful and achievable.

2) Performance feedback: Throughout the year, employees receive regular feedback on their performance from their managers and peers. This feedback is used to identify areas for improvement and provide coaching and support.

3) Performance evaluation: At the end of the year, managers evaluate each employee's performance against the goals they set at the beginning of the year. This evaluation is based on objective criteria, such as the completion of specific tasks or the achievement of specific outcomes.

4) Performance recognition: Employees who meet or exceed their goals are recognized and rewarded for their performance. This recognition may take the form of bonuses, promotions, or other forms of compensation.

TISCO's performance management system has been credited with improving employee engagement, motivation, and productivity. The system has also helped the company achieve its strategic objectives by aligning individual and team goals with the company's overall goals.

In addition to its performance management system, TISCO has also implemented several other innovative HR practices, such as employee training and development programs, employee engagement initiatives, and talent management strategies. These practices have helped the company build a culture of continuous improvement and innovation, and they have contributed to its success as a leading steel manufacturer in India and around the world.

1.8 Summary

1) The goal of performance management is to improve organizational performance by improving the performance of employees.

2) There are two types of performance management. The first focuses on the performance of an organization as a whole and evaluates the effectiveness of its managers. Second, it is about evaluating employees to ensure that they achieve reasonable objectives and, as a result, the organization performs better.

3) The performance management process aims to clarify performance objectives, standards, and critical dimensions in order to enhance individual performance.

4) An organization's performance management program is a systematic and holistic approach to identifying critical performance dimensions and implementing activities to ensure that it achieves its mission, objectives, goals, vision, and values effectively and efficiently.

5) The purpose of performance management is to translate organizational objectives and strategies into measurable actions. In order to accomplish this, it is important that the right information is provided to and received from the right people at the right time in the right format.

6) Integrated approaches to performance management are used in best-practice companies, not because performance management is a better technique than performance appraisal.

1.9 Keywords

• Expectancy: It refers to the likelihood that one's efforts will lead to the first level outcome.

• Instrumentality: It refers to the probabilities attached by the individual to each possible

• Likewise, the individual previously assigned probabilities to various levels of effort that result in different performance outcomes.

• Performance Management: It deals with improving organizational performance by improving employee performance.

• Performance: Behaviours or actions relevant to the organisation's goals.

• Valence: It means the attraction or outcome to an individual.

1.10 Self-Assessment

Fill in the blanks:

1. Performance deals with behaviour and......................

2. Performance management is .... in concept.

3. Performance is best developed through .... and experience.

4. .... is a systematic evaluation of present potential capabilities of personnel and employees by their superiors, superior's or a professional form outside.

5. The performance management approach focuses more on .... and concrete results based on the previously established smart objectives.

6. Performance management is a much broader term in comparison with ....

7. MBO means ....

8. Performance management may be considered a ....

State whether the following statements are true or false:

9. Performance management translates organizational objectives into work units, departmental teams and individual goals.

10. Performance management is a continuous and integrated process.

11. In the present scenario, organizations have shifted their focus from performance management to performance appraisals.

12. Performance management focuses on top-down assessment.

13. Performance appraisal is not directly linked to pay.

14. Performance management creates a system of regular feedback with positive reinforcement of employee's behaviour and action.

15. Performance management is more of a developmental tool rather than administration of financial rewards.

Answers: Self-Assessment

1. results 2. multidimensional

3. practical challenges 4. Performance appraisal

5. observed behaviours 6. performance appraisal

7. Management by Objectives 8. continuous process

9. True 10. True

11. False 12. False

13. False 14. True

15. True

1.11 Review Questions

1. Describe the concept of performance management.

2. "Performance management is key to success." Do you agree?

3. Analyze the philosophy behind performance management.

4. What are the pre-requisites of performance management?

5. List the key challenges to performance management.

6. What are the key reasons behind the move from performance appraisal to performance management?

7. Enlist performance management characteristics.

8. What are the key objectives and principles of performance management?

9. "Performance management helps employees evaluate themselves to achieve reasonable goals." Discuss.

10. Explain the linkage of performance management to other sub-systems.

CHAPTER TWO

Performance Management System

Objectives

Upon completion of this unit, you can:

• Describe the objectives and functions of a performance management system

• Analyze the characteristics of an effective project management system

• Defining competency-based project management systems

• Discuss the electronic performance management system

Introduction

The performance management system is another way of looking at a manager's overall responsibilities. The managerial function is viewed holistically as opposed to being recognized by managers and undertaken as their core function. Thus, management activities acquire a systemic dimension by emphasizing their interrelatedness and interdependence. Among these activities, it stresses their dynamic, sequential, and cyclical nature, essential to actualizing their synergistic potential. The source of high performance and excellence lies here. Furthermore, it explains why concentrating on only one or two of these activities won't deliver desired results.

To function smoothly, any system must meet certain prerequisites. PMS does the same. It is easier and more productive to use a PMS if:

1. Holistically, it is used in a systematic way

2. All relevant subsystems have been implemented and accepted

3. Having a philosophy and a work environment that promotes high morale is important to the organization

4. In addition to high performance attitudes, the manager is also equipped with leadership skills.

2.1 Objectives of Performance Management System

The primary objectives of a performance management system are to improve employee performance and achieve organizational goals. Below are some of the specific objectives of a performance management system:

1) Align individual and team goals with the organization's strategic objectives: A performance management system helps to ensure that individual and team goals are aligned with the overall goals of the organization. This helps to ensure that employees are working towards achieving the organization's objectives.

2) Improve employee performance: By setting clear expectations, providing regular feedback and coaching, and recognizing and rewarding good performance, a performance management system can help to improve employee performance.

3) Identify areas for improvement: A performance management system provides a framework for identifying areas where employees need to improve their skills, knowledge, or performance. This allows managers to provide targeted training and development opportunities to improve performance.

4) Support career development: A performance management system can provide employees with opportunities to develop their skills and knowledge and advance their careers within the organization.

5) Improve communication: A performance management system can improve communication between employees and their managers, as well as between different departments within the organization.

6) Increase employee engagement: By involving employees in the performance management process and recognizing and rewarding good performance, a performance management system can help to increase employee engagement and motivation.

7) Support organizational change: A performance management system can help to support organizational change by aligning individual and team goals with the new direction of the organization and by providing a framework for monitoring progress towards achieving the change.

In a nutshell, a performance management system is an important tool for organizations to improve performance, achieve their objectives, and support the development and engagement of their employees.

A company that uses performance management does not do so because it is a better method than performance appraisal, but because it can be integrated with other performance management methods. As a holistic approach, performance management contributes to the success of any organization by encompassing every aspect of business and giving those involved meaning and purpose.

2.2 Functions of Performance Management System

The functions of a Performance Management System (PMS) can be categorized into four main areas:

1) Goal Setting: This function involves setting clear and measurable performance goals and expectations for employees. Goals should be aligned with the organizational objectives and should be specific, measurable, achievable, relevant, and time-bound (SMART).

2) Performance Monitoring and Feedback: This function involves monitoring employee performance on an ongoing basis and providing regular feedback to employees. Performance feedback should be timely, specific, and focused on both positive aspects of performance and areas for improvement.

3) Performance Evaluation: This function involves formally evaluating employee performance at specific intervals, such as annually or bi-annually. Evaluation should be based on objective criteria and should consider both qualitative and quantitative aspects of performance.

4) Performance Improvement: This function involves identifying areas where employees need to improve their skills, knowledge, or performance and providing them with opportunities for training, coaching, and development. Performance improvement plans should be developed in collaboration with employees and should be focused on improving performance in areas that are critical to achieving organizational objectives.

Generally, the functions of a PMS are designed to improve employee performance, support the achievement of organizational objectives, and facilitate the development and engagement of employees.

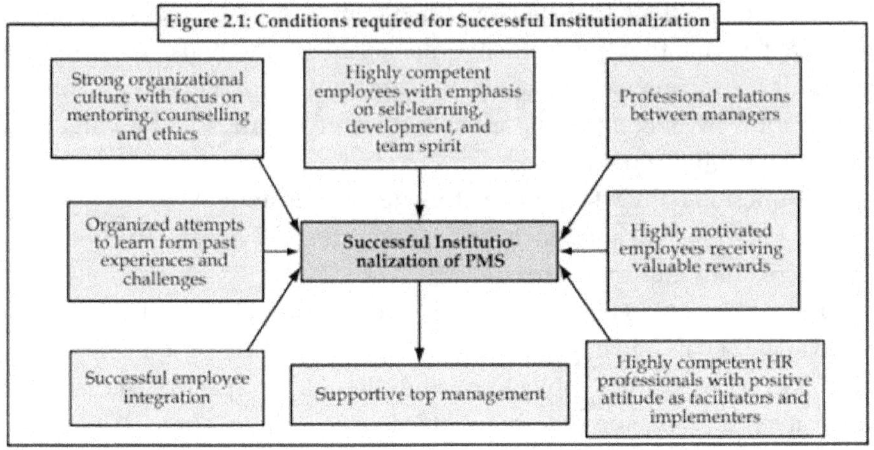

Enter Caption

2.3 Characteristics of Effective PMS

Effective Performance Management System (PMS) should have the following characteristics:

1) Clear and specific goals: Goals should be clear, specific, and aligned with the organization's strategic objectives. Employees should understand what is expected of them and how their performance will be measured.

2) Regular communication and feedback: Managers should provide regular feedback to employees on their performance, rather than waiting for formal evaluations. Communication should be open and honest, and managers should listen actively to employees' feedback.

3) Performance measurement: Performance measures should be objective, relevant, and reliable. They should provide meaningful information on employee performance and should be linked to the organization's strategic objectives.

4) Employee development: Effective PMS should focus on employee development by identifying opportunities for training, coaching, and career advancement. Employees should be provided with the necessary resources and support to develop their skills and knowledge.

5) Employee involvement: Employees should be involved in the performance management process. This can be achieved by involving employees in setting goals, providing feedback, and evaluating their own

performance.

6) Fairness and equity: PMS should be fair and equitable. Performance evaluations should be based on objective criteria, and employees should be evaluated against the same standards. Managers should also consider the impact of external factors on employee performance.

7) Continuous improvement: Effective PMS should be continuously reviewed and improved to ensure that it remains relevant and effective. Managers should seek feedback from employees and evaluate the effectiveness of the PMS on a regular basis.

As a whole, an effective PMS should support the achievement of organizational objectives, improve employee performance, and facilitate the development and engagement of employees.

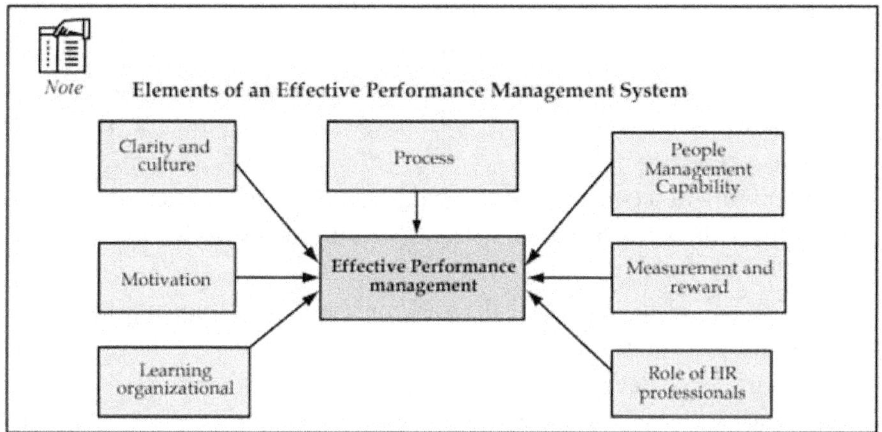

Figure 2.2

2.4 Competency-based PMS

Competency-based Performance Management System (PMS) is an approach that focuses on identifying and developing employee competencies that are critical to achieving organizational objectives. Competencies are the knowledge, skills, abilities, and behaviours that employees need to perform their job successfully.

In a competency-based PMS, job roles and responsibilities are defined in terms of the competencies required to perform them. These competencies are identified through job analysis and are used as a basis for setting performance expectations and evaluating employee performance.

The key features of a competency-based PMS are:

1) Competency framework: A competency framework is developed, which identifies the competencies required for different job roles and levels within the organization.

2) Competency assessment: Competency assessment is conducted to identify the strengths and development needs of employees in relation to the competencies required for their job roles.

3) Competency-based performance planning: Performance expectations are set based on the competencies required for the job role, and development plans are developed to address any competency gaps.

4) Competency-based performance evaluation: Employee performance is evaluated based on the competencies required for their job role, rather than just the quantity or quality of their work.

5) Competency-based feedback and coaching: Feedback and coaching are provided to employees on their performance in relation to the competencies required for their job role, and development plans are adjusted as needed.

The benefits of a competency-based PMS are that it helps to:

1) Align individual performance with organizational objectives

2) Identify and develop critical competencies

3) Provide a clear framework for performance expectations and development planning

4) Foster employee development and engagement

5) Encourage ongoing feedback and coaching

In a nutshell, a competency-based PMS is a valuable approach for organizations that want to focus on developing the skills and knowledge of their employees and aligning individual performance with organizational objectives.

Competency

Competencies are the knowledge, skills, and personal characteristics required for successful performance in a specific job, role, or enterprise.

An organization's competency development process is the process of gathering data and conducting research about its managers and employees as they carry out their daily tasks, with the objective of determining the specific skills, knowledge, and personal attributes needed to perform at these actual jobs, roles, or businesses well.

The competencies and the need for development translate into personal development plans. The whole links into what is being tried within the organization. As defined by Severn Trent Water, competency is a set of knowledge, skills, and behaviours that may be required in whole or in part in a variety of managerial situations. A competency analysis examines the behavioural dimensions of a role.

Figure 2.3

Lockett (1992) says, "The essence of performance management is the development of individuals with competence and commitment, working towards the achievement of shared meaningful objectives within an organization that supports and encourages their achievement."

Performance management is concerned with creating a culture in which organizational and individual learning and development are continuous. It provides means for the integration of learning and work so that everyone learns from the successes and challenges inherent in their day-to-day activities. The drive to enhance performance is making ever-greater demands on the knowledge and skills of the workforce and on people, who carry much more significant responsibility for their own performance.

Team performance management deserves more attention. What makes an effective team, the competencies required for teamwork and a definition of what can be considered a team for performance management purposes? Peer pressure in teamwork is important.

Project teams that are tightly knit and have a long history are critical to performance management.

According to Hay/McBer (Gross 1995), some of the key competencies for teamwork are:

1. Interpersonal Understanding
2. Influence
3. Customer Service Orientation
4. Adaptability
5. Team Work
6. Oral Communication
7. Achievement Orientation
8. Organizational Commitment

For teams, performance measurement will be based on their purposes, objectives, and standards.

Performance Management System Checklist for Managing

1. Do you have written performance standards for the employees? Yes/No
2. Have you communicated the performance standards to the employees? Yes/No
3. Are the standards clear and reasonable? Yes/No
4. Has HR representative reviewed the standards for any possible problems? Yes/No
5. Have you told the employee what critical element he is failing in? Yes/No
6. Have you counselled the employee on how to improve to an acceptable level? Yes/No
7. Have you fully assessed and utilized all available resources to help the employee Yes/No
8. improve? Have you explained and offered them to the employee? Yes/No
9. Have you sought employee input regarding what is needed to improve? Yes/No

10. Have interim review periods been established to measure the employee's improvement? Yes/No
11. Have you advised the employee what he has to do to improve performance and retain the job? Yes/No
12. Have you provided all the agreed assistance including training to the employee? Yes/No
13. Did you consider any requests for accommodation? Yes/No
14. Have you taken into account annual, sick, or to her leave taken during the review periods? Yes/No
15. Did you document the employee's performance, your efforts to assist, the employee's actions and contributions to the improvement plan, etc.? Yes/No
16. Do you have copies of any notes of counselling and/or assistance to the employee? Yes/No
17. Do you have copies of memoranda of counselling provided to the employee? Yes/No
18. Has there been due process prior to the administration of any discipline? Yes/No
19. Do you have a just cause to administer progressive discipline and/or use the alternate discipline process, and the document to demonstrate the just cause. Yes/No

2.5 Electronic Performance Management

Electronic performance management (or E-performance management) offers significant value for money to organizations and addresses their needs. With electronic performance management, you can integrate the organization's metrics with an online software package. It provides greater flexibility, tracking, and access to performance management to a large number of employees and managers across the organization, and across the world. This is at the press of a button. Bititci et al. As (2000) points out, using an IT platform for managing performance management within an organization simplifies the maintenance of information contained within these systems. They also set up some requirements for an IT platform, suitable for such a situation. This e-performance management software is readily available as standard product, or can be customized to meet a specific need of the organization.

The E-performance management product allows organizations to maintain a record of core skills and competencies into the employee's performance management process. E-performance management provides templates for a wide application that could be used across organizations spread in different parts of the world through one software module. E-performance management templates provide the following features:

1. Job – or individual – cantered performance contracts
2. Uploading of performance criteria
3. Secure online appraisal with password
4. Automatic e-mail notification of completed appraisal to employee and manager
5. Workflow system to monitor appraisal progress
6. Archive retrieval possible for retrieval of previous period appraisals
7. Assigning different weighting protocols
8. Viewing competency ratings
9. Viewing compensation details
10. Career advancement and opportunities available

Implementing performance management across an organization creates the potential for large administrative overhead. Performance management processes must be completed and approved, feedback and counselling must be provided from multiple reviewers, documents rated, deadlines monitored, and many of these activities must be performed multiple times during each performance cycle for each and every employee. E-performance management (e.g., Oracle's PeopleSoft Applications) helps organizations automate many administrative processes surrounding performance management. E-performance management enables rule-based routing of performance documents for editing and approval, the delivered language editor and results writer tools enable standardized content to be suggested at the time of appraisal, and the status dashboard enables all parties to track their documents as they move through the performance management process, that is, from planning to monitoring and beyond.

E-performance management offers numerous benefits, including:

For Managers:

1. Focused and aligned performance goals directly influence organizational performance

2. Employee performance and focus areas are accessible instantly

3. Performance management is a key part of an organization's integrated human resource strategy

4. Easy to drill down through performance data for root cause analyses for marginal performers

5. Get instant feedback on performance with drill down to individual employee performance

6. No need to write performance contracts each year. Simply upload and edit from a previous period

7. Development needs that arise from performance discussions are automatically incorporated into the individual development plan.

For HR Professionals:

Organization-wide quality assurance of goals and Key Performance Indicators (KPIs).

e-performance Management Practices in Indian Organisations

Technology has changed the face of business. Many HR transactions have been automated especially performance management. We now look at IT-enabled performance management practices of some leading companies in India.

- At **Nokia India**, there are no performance appraisal forms. Performance criteria are set by employee in concurrence with his manager in the appraisal tool. Reviewing officer reviews the same. This tool helps to update the goal setting and achievements periodically.

- At **PepsiCo**, employees unload their performance targets on MDN, a global portal which is available to PepsiCo employees across the world. Mid-term review and final appraisals facilities by MDN, also guides employees in tracking their career plans by preparing Career Development Action Plan. The data is subsequently used by HR.

At **TCS**, managers use an online system for carrying out performance management system, merit pay, and succession planning activities with ease.

1. Progress of goal/KPI setting and appraisal is monitored and managed

2. Monitor appraisal bias within the organization

3. Paper-based forms are eliminated, making process management more efficient and secure

4. Managers are more likely to conduct effective goal/KPI setting and appraisal, given ease of use

5. Performance management more likely to become entrenched in the organization.

We conclude in the words of Agha Husan Abedi:

"The conventional definition of management is getting work done through people, but real management is developing people through work."

2.6 Summary

- Performance management system is another way of envisioning the totality of a manager's function.
- The use of performance management in the best-practice companies is not because it is a better technique than performance appraisal, but because it can form one of a number of integrated approaches to the management of performance.
- The rise of HRM also contributed to the emergence of performance management.
- PMS helps in clarifying the mission, vision, strategy, and values of the organization to the employees in order to enable them achieve the same.
- Companies use performance management systems to evaluate employees' efficiency at work and ability to perform certain tasks, either by automated or human processes.
- Competency development is a carefully crafted process of research and data-gathering about fi rm's managers and employees as they perform their daily work, with the goal of determining the specific knowledge, skills and personal attributes required for excellent performance in these actual jobs, roles or businesses.
- The competencies and the need to develop them translates into a personal development plan and the whole links into what is being tried to be achieved within the organization.
- Electronic performance management (or e-performance management) offers great value for money to the organizations and addresses its needs aptly.
- The e-performance management product allows organizations to maintain a record of core skills and competencies into the employee's performance management process.

2.7 Keywords

- Competencies: Competencies are the knowledge, skills and personal attributes required for excellent performance in a job, role or specific business.

- Competency analysis: Competency analysis is concerned with the behavioural dimensions of the roles.
- e-performance Management: It is IT-enabled performance management that comes as an effective tool to leverage the full benefits of the system at a comparatively much lesser cost of administration.
- Performance Management: It deals with improving organizational performance by improving employee performance.

2.8 Self-Assessment

Fill in the blanks:

1. In the organization with performance management systems, ... had performance pay and 76 percent rated performance.

2. The goals and objectives of an organisation determine the organizational ....

3. .... offers the same benefits of system of performance management at a much lower cost.

4. .... is perhaps the most important function of performance management.

5. Performance management is regarded as a number of .... processes rather than a single system.

6. .... are the knowledge, skills and personal attributes required for excellent performance in a job, role or specific business.

7. .... is concerned with the behavioural dimensions of the roles.

8. Performance management is concerned with creating a culture in which organizational and individual learning and development are a ....

9. The performance management for .... deserves more attention.

10. The .... product allows organizations to maintain a record of core skills and competencies into the employee's performance management process.

State whether the following statements are true or false:

11. Implementing performance management across and organization creates the potential for a large amount of administrative overhead.

12. e-performance management enables rule-based routing of performance documents for editing and approval.

13. Performance management processes are not effective in tightly knit and long-standing project teams.

14. Performance management is not concerned with outputs.

15. An effective PMS link performance requirement to pay, especially for senior managers.

Answers: Self-Assessment

1. 85 percent 2. strategy

3. e-performance management 4. Development

5. inter-linked 6. Competencies

7. Competency analysis 8. continuous process

9. teams 10. e-performance management

11. True 12. True

13. False 14. False

15. True

2.9 Review Questions

1. Do you think that performance management system is more successful in large organisations in comparison to the smaller one? Discuss.

2. Performance management system is an inter-linked process. Defi ne the statement by giving some practical examples.

3. Why do different organisations have different performance management system, although the principles of performance management system are same?

4. "Performance management should be a continuous process". In light of this statement, discuss the features of a good performance management system.

5. Why do organisations opt for performance management?

6. What do you mean by employee performance? How can performance be bettered?

7. "Any system needs certain prerequisites to function smoothly." Discuss the statement with respect PMS.

8. Companies use performance management systems to evaluate employees' efficiency at work and ability to perform certain tasks, either by automated or human processes. If you are the HR manager of your organisation then how you will develop an effective performance management system for your organisation.

9. "A PMS helps in clarifying the mission, vision, strategy, and values of the organization to the employees in order to enable them achieve the same." Discuss.

10. According to Lockett (1992), "The essence of performance management is the development of individuals with competence and commitment,

working towards the achievement of shared meaningful objectives within an organization which supports and encourages their achievement." Define

CHAPTER THREE

Performance Planning

Objectives

After studying this unit, you can:
   • Describe the characteristics and objectives of performance planning
• Analyze performance planning's importance and methodology
• The process of performance planning and its barriers

Introduction

The performance-planning part of the performance-management sequence is primarily a joint exploration of what individuals need to do and know to improve their performance and develop their skills and competences, and how their managers can provide the support and guidance they need. This requires competency mapping & Development of Machines & Potentials.

The performance aspect of the plan facilitated agreement on what must be done to achieve objectives, raise standards and improve performance. It also establishes priorities—the key aspects of the job to which attention must be given. Agreement is also reached at this stage on the basis upon which performance will be measured. In addition, the evidence used to establish levels of competence. It is imperative that these measures and evidence requirements are identified and fully agreed now. This is because they will be used jointly by managers and individuals and collectively by teams to monitor progress and demonstrate achievements.

In other words, Performance planning is the process of setting goals and objectives for an individual or organization, determining the actions necessary to achieve those goals, and identifying the resources required to complete those actions. This process can be used to improve the overall performance of an individual or team by providing a clear direction for their efforts and ensuring that their actions are aligned with the organization's goals and objectives.

Effective performance planning involves setting specific, measurable, achievable, relevant, and time-bound (SMART) goals and objectives that are aligned with the organization's strategic objectives. It also requires identifying the key performance indicators (KPIs) that will be used to measure progress towards those goals and objectives, and establishing a system for monitoring and reporting on progress.

Performance planning can be used at various levels within an organization, from individual employee performance plans to departmental or organizational performance plans. By providing a clear roadmap for achieving goals and objectives, performance planning can help to improve motivation, accountability, and overall performance.

3.1 Characteristics of Performance Planning

The following are the key characteristics of effective performance planning:

a) Clear goals and objectives: Performance planning involves setting clear and specific goals and objectives that are aligned with the organization's strategic objectives. These goals and objectives should be challenging yet achievable and measurable.

b) Collaboration and communication: Performance planning is a collaborative process that involves input from all stakeholders. Effective communication is essential to ensure that everyone is on the same page and understands their roles and responsibilities.

c) Regular feedback and review: Regular feedback and review are critical components of performance planning. This allows for ongoing monitoring and adjustment of goals and objectives based on progress towards achieving them.

d) Resource allocation: Performance planning requires the allocation of the necessary resources, including people, time, and budget, to achieve the goals and objectives.

e) Alignment with organizational strategy: Performance planning should be aligned with the organization's overall strategy and objectives. This ensures that all efforts are focused on achieving the organization's strategic goals.

f) Continuous improvement: Performance planning is an ongoing process of continuous improvement. It involves identifying areas for improvement and taking action to address them.

g) Results-oriented: Performance planning is results-oriented, focusing on achieving specific outcomes and measurable results. KPIs are used to track progress and measure success.

In a nutshell, effective performance planning is a dynamic and ongoing process that requires collaboration, communication, and continuous improvement. It is results-oriented and aligned with the organization's overall strategy and objectives.

3.2 Objectives of Performance Planning

The primary objectives of performance planning are to:

a) Establish clear and specific goals and objectives: Performance planning helps to define the specific goals and objectives that an individual or team needs to achieve. This provides clarity and focus, which helps to align efforts towards a common purpose.

b) Align individual and organizational objectives: Performance planning ensures that individual objectives are aligned with the organization's overall strategy and objectives. This helps to ensure that everyone is working towards a common goal, which is essential for the success of the organization.

c) Improve performance: Performance planning provides a framework for improving individual and team performance. It sets clear expectations, provides feedback and support, and encourages continuous improvement.

d) Increase motivation and engagement: By involving individuals and teams in the performance planning process, they become more engaged and invested in achieving the goals and objectives. This can increase motivation, job satisfaction, and overall performance.

e) Enhance communication: Performance planning involves regular communication and feedback between managers and employees. This can enhance communication and build stronger relationships between team members.

f) Identify development opportunities: Performance planning helps to identify individual and team development needs. This can lead to targeted training and development programs that help to build skills and capabilities.

Generally, the objectives of performance planning are to improve individual and team performance, align individual objectives with organizational objectives, increase motivation and engagement, and identify development opportunities. This helps to build a more effective and efficient organization that is better able to achieve its strategic objectives.

Best practice identifies that objectives are easily understood and acted upon when they are specific, measurable, achievable, realistic and time specific. The acronym SMART helps remember those components.

To set SMART objectives it is imperative to:

1. Identify the expected outcome, the 'what';

2. Provide indicators to measure achievement;

3. Create an objective that is a challenge within the staff member's capabilities;

4. Take into account available resources; and

5. Include a target date or response time.

3.3 Importance of Performance Planning

Performance planning is important for several reasons:

Provides clarity and focus: Performance planning helps to provide clarity and focus on what needs to be achieved. It sets clear expectations, goals, and objectives that align with the organization's overall strategy. This helps to ensure that everyone is working towards a common purpose.

a) Improves performance: Performance planning provides a framework for improving individual and team performance. It sets clear goals and objectives, provides feedback and support, and encourages continuous improvement. This helps to improve the performance of individuals and teams.

b) Enhances communication: Performance planning involves regular communication and feedback between managers and employees. This can enhance communication and build stronger relationships between team members. This can help to improve collaboration, teamwork, and overall performance.

c) Aligns individual and organizational objectives: Performance planning ensures that individual objectives are aligned with the organization's overall strategy and objectives. This helps to ensure that everyone is working towards a common goal, which is essential for the success of the organization.

d) Identifies development opportunities: Performance planning helps to identify individual and team development needs. This can lead to targeted training and development programs that help to build skills and capabilities.

e) Increases motivation and engagement: By involving individuals and teams in the performance planning process, they become more engaged and invested in achieving the goals and objectives. This can increase motivation, job satisfaction, and overall performance.

In summary, performance planning is important because it provides clarity and focus, improves performance, enhances communication, aligns individual and organizational objectives, identifies development opportunities, and increases motivation and engagement. These benefits help to build a more effective and efficient organization that is better able to achieve its strategic objectives.

3.4 Methodologies of Performance Planning

There are several methodologies of performance planning, including:

a) Management by objectives (MBO): MBO is a goal-setting methodology that involves defining specific, measurable, achievable, relevant, and time-bound (SMART) goals and objectives. This methodology involves a collaborative process between managers and employees to set individual goals that are aligned with the organization's overall objectives.

b) Performance-based planning: Performance-based planning is a methodology that focuses on outcomes and results. This methodology involves setting performance targets and measures, developing strategies to achieve those targets, and monitoring progress towards achieving those targets.

c) Balanced scorecard: The balanced scorecard is a methodology that involves setting objectives and measures across four perspectives: financial, customer, internal processes, and learning and growth. This methodology is designed to ensure that organizational objectives are balanced across different areas, and that performance is measured in a holistic way.

d) Six Sigma: Six Sigma is a methodology that focuses on process improvement and reducing defects or errors. This methodology involves setting goals to improve process efficiency and effectiveness, and measuring progress towards achieving those goals.

e) Agile performance management: Agile performance management is a methodology that focuses on continuous feedback and improvement. This methodology involves setting short-term goals, providing regular feedback, and adjusting goals and objectives based on progress towards achieving them.

In general, the choice of methodology will depend on the organization's specific needs and goals. The most effective performance planning methodologies are those that are aligned with the organization's overall strategy and objectives, and that provide a clear framework for improving individual and team performance.

Performance criteria should be set up based on the following methodologies:

1. Key performance area
2. Key results area

3. Task and target identification

4. Goal setting exercises

5. Organizational objectives and strategy

6. Assessment of organizational performance needs

7. Setting organizational performance expectations

8. Establishing a performance management process

9. Measuring performance management effectiveness

1. Key Performance Area: An employee's key performance area includes identifying the priority area and subsequently working on it. The process of determining key performance areas involves the following steps:

(a) Identification of significant tasks and activities

(b) Determine the priority area

(c) Setting goals in the identified area

(d) Seeking employee commitment to identified work

(e) Making arrangements for the required resources

2. Key Results Area: The term key results area is a general area of outcomes for which a role is responsible. Identifying KRAs helps individual employees in a number of ways as enumerated here:

(a) Clarify their roles.

(b) Align their roles with the organization's business or strategic plan.

(c) Focus on results rather than activities.

(d) Communicate their role's purpose to others.

(e) Set goals and objectives.

(f) Prioritize their activities, and improve their time/work management.

(g) Make value-added decisions. Key areas of a work role capture about 80 percent of a work role. The remainder of the role is usually devoted to shared responsibility.

Example:

An organization's image is usually a key outcome area for a very senior official, but it is assumed that every employee plays a role in improving it.

The key results areas are worded in as few terms as possible, without verbs, stating results, not actions, and without direction/measurement. They simply describe the areas in which one is responsible for results.

Individuals undertake the following steps to determine the KRAs for their roles

(a) Enlist the main day-to-day responsibilities/activities.

(b) For each activity, ask 'Why do I do this?'

(c) Review the answers to the 'why' questions, looking for common themes or areas.

(d) Identify KRAs from these themes.

(e) Share KRAs, preferably with those they report to, those they work with, and those who report to them.

The KRA approach has three main advantages:

(a) Areas such as innovation, customer response time, and employee development are included rather than overlooked.

(b) It is the first step in setting objectives.

(c) It makes it easier to assess current performance.

3.Tasks and Target Identification: Tasks and target identification involves the identification of the roles, responsibilities, tasks and key targets of employees. Employees should know their duties and key targets.

4. Goal Setting Exercises: An organization's ultimate goals determine its strategy.

Example: An organization intending to become the world's largest textile company in the shortest possible time (ultimate goal) will increase its production capacities either through an organic route such as setting up new manufacturing facilities, or by acquiring other textile organizations. Since acquisition helps increase production capacities quickly, the organization shall pursue acquisition as a strategy for faster growth. But the acquisition strategy also involves turning around the performance of older acquired production units. This essentially calls for improving human performance for corporate success.

5. Organizational objectives and strategy:

(a) An organization's ultimate goal

(b) The organization's competitive position

(c) Comparing an organization's strength with a changing environment

(d) Examining the organization's critical issues

(e) Analysing the organization's opportunities

(f) Exploring appropriate approaches to organizational resources and competencies

6. Assessment of organizational performance needs:

(a) Identifying competencies necessary for achieving organizational objectives and strategy (b) Gathering information about critical issues

(c) Determine the current and future performance needs

(d) Prioritizing organizational improvement measures

(e) Recognizing core organizational values

7. Setting organizational performance expectations:

(a) Determine required vs. desired performance

(b) Determine current performance status

(c) Understanding, aligning, and agreeing on performance expectations

(d) Formulating key performance indicators

(e) Evolving job objectives (f) Aligning individual goals with organizational strategy

8. Establishing a performance management process:

(a) Designing a performance management framework

(b) Performance planning

(c) Performance managing

(d) Performance appraisal

(e) Performance monitoring

9. Measuring performance management effectiveness:

(a) Identifying performance development opportunities

(b) Providing performance counselling including 360-degree feedback

(c) Devising reward strategies and administering a reward system

(d) Instituting performance management audit

(e) Improvement in the competitive position of the organization

3.5 Process of Performance Planning

The process of performance planning typically involves the following steps:

a) Defining goals and objectives: The first step in performance planning is to define the specific goals and objectives that the individual or team needs to achieve. These goals should be specific, measurable, achievable, relevant, and time-bound (SMART).

b) Aligning goals with organizational objectives: Once goals and objectives have been defined, it's important to ensure that they are aligned with the organization's overall strategy and objectives. This helps to ensure that everyone is working towards a common goal.

c) Identifying performance measures: Performance measures are used to track progress towards achieving goals and objectives. These measures should be specific, relevant, and easily measurable.

d) Developing an action plan: Once goals and objectives have been defined and performance measures identified, it's important to develop an action plan to achieve those goals. This plan should outline the specific steps that need to be taken to achieve the goals and objectives.

e) Assigning responsibilities: Each member of the team should have clearly defined responsibilities for achieving the goals and objectives. This helps to ensure accountability and ensure that everyone is working towards a common goal.

f) Providing feedback and support: Regular feedback and support are essential for achieving goals and objectives. Managers should provide feedback to team members on their progress towards achieving goals, and provide support as needed.

g) Monitoring progress: Regular monitoring of progress towards achieving goals and objectives is important to ensure that the action plan is on track. This helps to identify any issues or challenges that may arise, and make necessary adjustments to the action plan.

h) Reviewing and evaluating: Finally, it's important to review and evaluate performance planning periodically to determine its effectiveness. This helps to identify areas for improvement and make necessary adjustments to the process.

Generally, the process of performance planning involves defining goals and objectives, aligning them with organizational objectives, identifying performance measures, developing an action plan, assigning responsibilities, providing feedback and support, monitoring progress, and reviewing and evaluating the process.

Supervisors and employees benefit from an effective performance planning and review process. The process should identify clearly what is expected of an employee. This in turn provides the opportunity to recognize positive performance and recognize areas that need corrective action or added training. Four areas must be identified in a performance plan:

1. Job responsibility – What must be done?

2. Performance measures – How will this be checked or measured?

3. Performance standard – How well must it be done?

4. Target date – When will it be checked?

When building a performance plan, you would obtain information in these areas from the job description. You would also look to the organization needs to clarify which duties have priority and the standard they must be performed to. An effective performance plan should outline results expected, performance measures, standards to be achieved and target dates for measurement.

Performance planning includes the following key components:

1. Preparation of Performance Plans: Performance plans are usually prepared at the beginning of the annual review period, or when an employee starts their new job. Preparing for the initial planning meeting

should be undertaken by both the supervisor and the employee. Both supervisor and employee should review the goals, objectives and needs of the work unit and looking at the current job description. The supervisor should list the things in the job they intend to measure, and the standards you will measure to. The employee could write down the ways each of their tasks could be measured and how well each should be performed.

2. Identification of Key Success Factors: Priority and focus should be placed on performance objectives and results to be achieved. Measures should be specific to each task, with clear standards including dates and times when appropriate.

3. Setting Departmental and Individual Objectives: After setting the organisational goals and objectives the departmental goals and objectives are defined. The departmental objectives are further categorised into individual goals. Individual goals include key duties and responsibilities to achieve the organization's ultimate goals.

4. Providing Regular Feedback: The next step in the process is providing regular feedback. The supervisor should maintain a log of performance facts. This will ensure that significant issues are given the attention required and will help the formal review proceed in a more focused and potentially more positive way. The employee should also maintain a record of accomplishments and special achievements, or issues that need to be resolved. Discussion of these things during scheduled or spontaneous feedback sessions will resolve problems quickly.

5. Performance Review: Reviewing performance gives the supervisor and the employee the opportunity to look at results achieved in relation to the original plan and standards of performance established. At this meeting, you should assess all performance records and each task. You should discuss whether they met the performance standards or not, and whether they exceeded those standards. Review any outside factors that may have affected performance. At this time, the supervisor should identify any areas where improvement may be necessary or performance could be enhanced. The employee should also have the opportunity to discuss areas where they could use more help.

6. Action Planning: Another critical aspect of completing this cycle is action planning. This is where the supervisor and employee would plan for any training that needs to occur, and could also be where you discuss career planning.

In Eicher Motors Ltd, make a discussion about performance planning.

3.6 Barriers to Performance Planning

There are several barriers that can prevent effective performance planning, including:

a) Lack of clear direction: If employees are unclear about their goals and objectives, it can be difficult for them to know what they need to achieve. This can lead to confusion and lack of direction, which can prevent effective performance planning.

b) Poor communication: Effective performance planning requires clear and regular communication between managers and employees. If communication is poor, it can lead to misunderstandings and misaligned goals, which can prevent effective performance planning.

c) Limited resources: Limited resources, such as time, budget, and staff, can prevent effective performance planning. Without adequate resources, it can be difficult to develop and implement effective performance planning processes.

d) Resistance to change: Some employees may be resistant to change, which can prevent effective performance planning. This resistance can be due to fear of the unknown, lack of trust in management, or simply a preference for the status quo.

e) Lack of buy-in: Effective performance planning requires buy-in from both managers and employees. If either group is not fully committed to the process, it can prevent effective performance planning.

f) Lack of accountability: Without clear accountability for achieving goals and objectives, it can be difficult to motivate employees to perform at their best. This lack of accountability can prevent effective performance planning.

In general, effective performance planning requires clear direction, good communication, adequate resources, a willingness to change, buy-in from both managers and employees, and clear accountability for achieving goals and objectives. By addressing these barriers, organizations can develop and implement effective performance planning processes that drive success and achieve their strategic objectives.

Performance planning barriers can be categorised as follows:

1. **Organisational Barriers:** Most traditional organisations are against performance planning. According to these organisations spending time on performance planning is just wasted time. These organisations believe in strong implementation strategy.

Example: Indian companies tend to spend 30% of their time on planning and the remaining 70% on implementation. In contrast, MNCs usually spend 70% time on performance planning and the remaining 30% time on strategy implementation.

2. **Individual Barriers:** There are also individual barriers to performance planning, including lack of commitment among the organization's employees and management. Sometimes managers or employees or both show less commitment to organisational goals. The reasons could be personal, organisational, competitive or any other HR factor.

Example: Organisational politics, workplace bullying or high conflict cause employees to show less interest in their job responsibilities.

Case Study: New Software to Improve Penrith Council's Planning

The Penrith City Council's objective was to effectively produce strategic and management plans, along with detailed project and activity plans as well as associated reporting. The Council required online reporting to replace its current hardcopy reporting and there was a strong desire by the Council to provide staff with an improved user experience and to increase productivity and skills in both planning and performance reporting. Tenders were called to replace the incumbent system in 2002. Four compliant tenders were received and after a rigorous evaluation process Outcome Manager (Technology One's performance planning solution) was selected. This performance planning solution was deemed to be the most efficient and effective tool and delivered the most flexibility for the Council. The Council recognised the system's ability to produce real productivity and transparency benefits by enabling tasks to be assigned, delegated, reassigned or shifted to different levels as well as enabling people on leave to temporarily assign items. Penrith City Council believed that a performance planning solution would enhance functionality in areas that were underdeveloped, such as cross-functional planning, project evaluation and both financial and capacity planning. At a grassroots level there was the desire to provide employees with a greater understanding of their roles within the Strategic and Management Plan framework and to demonstrate that the Council is efficient and effective within government as well as being customer focused. Integration and ease of use were key decision factors. Council saw this solution as the best choice because it could be deployed via a web browser, enabling the system to fit seamlessly with both the intranet and the Internet, which meant that staff working remotely could maintain access. Its flexibility and ability to adapt to the Council's needs, along with its compatibility with the Council's Microsoft SQL Server platform, were also integral to the selection process. "Council had a strong planning framework and reporting procedures, but until we implemented a performance planning solution, we lacked the system to bring it all together."

Ross Kingsley

Corporate Development Manager

Penrith City Council

Source: www.technologyonecorp.com

3.7 Summary

i. The performance-planning part of the performance-management sequence is primarily a joint exploration of what individuals need to do and know to improve their performance and develop their skills and competences, and how their managers can provide the support and guidance they need.

ii. The performance aspect of the plan obtained agreement on what must be done to achieve objectives, raise standards and improve performance.

iii. Performance planning is a key component of an effective performance management system.

iv. Coaches work with performance plans or work plans to keep employees motivated.

v. A key performance area includes identifying a priority area to an employee and addressing the area as soon as possible.

vi. The term key results area is a general area of outcomes for which a role is responsible.

vii. The process of performance planning should identify clearly what is expected of an employee. This in turn provides the opportunity to recognize positive performance and identify areas that need corrective action or added training

3.8 Keywords

Goal: The purpose toward which an endeavour is directed.

Mission: It defines what an organization is, why it exists, and its reason for being.

Objectives: Something one's efforts or actions are intended to attain or accomplish.

Performance: It's behaviour, but outcomes may be contaminated by systems factors, so it's important to distinguish it from them.

Vision: A statement giving a broad, inspirational image of the future an organization aims to achieve.

3.9 Self-Assessment

Fill in the blanks:

1. The performance aspect of the plan obtained agreement on what must be done to achieve objectives, raise .... and improve performance.

2. Performance planning is a .... which starts with understanding organisational objectives and ends with setting performance criteria.

3. Performance planning is an integral part of ....

4. .... includes the identifi cation of priority area to an employee and subsequent working on the specifi ed area.

5. The term key results area may be defined as .... of outcomes for which a role is responsible.

6. Key results areas capture about .... of a work role.

7. An organization's ultimate goals determine its ....

8. Performance objectives and results to be achieved should be focused on results and set in order of ....

9. Indian companies tend to spend 30% of their time on .... and the remaining 70% on implementation. State whether the following statements are true or false:

10. MNCs usually spend 60% time on performance planning and the remaining 40% time on strategy implementation.

11. Key results areas capture about 90 percent of a work role

Answers: Self-Assessment

1. standards 2. continuous process

3. performance management system 4. Key performance area

5. general area 6. 80 percent

7. strategy 8 priority

9. planning 10. False

11. False

3.10 Review Questions

1. Design a performance planning process for your organisation.

2. Is there any impact of performance planning on the company's mission, vision and objectives? Discuss.

3. "A performance plan establishes the development researcher's essential job tasks, responsibilities, and critical performance objectives that

need to be achieved or performed during the performance period." Discuss.

4. "Key results area areas capture about 80 percent of a work role." Define.

5. Identify and analyze the statement that an organization's ultimate goals determine its strategy.

6. In most Indian companies' performance management is limited up to performance appraisal. Discuss the key reasons.

7. "Indian companies tend to spend 30% of their time on planning and 70% on implementation. In contrast, MNCs usually spend 70% of their time on performance planning and 30% on strategy implementation." Discuss.

8. Identify the four areas to identify in a performance plan?

9. "An effective performance plan should outline the results expected, performance measures, standards to be achieved and target dates for measurement." Discuss.

10. "An organization intending to become the world's largest textile company in the shortest possible time (ultimate goal) will increase its production capacities either through organic routes such as setting up existing manufacturing facilities, or by acquiring other textile Organizations." Discuss.

CHAPTER FOUR

Competency Mapping

Objectives

As a result of studying this unit, you will be able to:
• Develop a competency mapping model
• Describe the methods for mapping competencies

Introduction

Competency mapping begins with identifying key competencies for an organization and/or a job. It incorporates those competencies throughout the various processes (i.e., job evaluation, training, recruitment) of the organization. With a competency-based job description, the second step involves mapping those competencies throughout the organization's human resources processes. The competencies of a job description are also considered when evaluating the performance of the individual. Using competencies helps evaluate objectively displayed or not displayed behaviours. Taking competency mapping one step further, performance evaluation results can be used to identify competencies individuals need additional development or training.

4.1 Building Competency Models

Competencies models may be developed in three ways:

1. Behavioural Indicators: Behavioural indicators describe behaviours, thought patterns, abilities and traits that contribute to superior performance.

2. Evaluative Competency Levels: Exceptional competencies of high performers are set as standards for evaluating employees' competency levels.

3. Competencies Describing Job Requirements: This approach is useful for organizations having multiple competency models. Competencies required for a particular job are described. Job specific competency models help structure focused appraisal and compensation decisions.

Competency models are an essential tool for organizations to identify and define the skills, behaviours, and knowledge necessary for success in a particular role or within the company as a whole. Competency models provide a framework for hiring, developing, and evaluating employees, as well as for providing feedback and coaching.

We will explore the process of building competency models, including the key steps and considerations.

1: Define the Purpose and Scope

The first step in building a competency model is to define the purpose and scope. This involves identifying the specific roles or functions that the competency model will apply to, as well as the intended outcomes. For example, an organization may want to develop a competency model for its sales team to improve performance and increase revenue.

2: Conduct a Job Analysis

The next step is to conduct a job analysis to identify the key competencies required for success in the identified roles or functions. This can be done through a variety of methods, such as interviews with subject matter experts, observation of job tasks, and analysis of job descriptions and performance data.

3: Identify Competencies

Based on the job analysis, the next step is to identify the specific competencies required for success in the identified roles or functions. Competencies can be grouped into categories such as technical skills, interpersonal skills, and leadership skills.

4: Define Competencies

Once the competencies have been identified, the next step is to define them. This involves creating a clear and concise description of each competency, including the behaviours, knowledge, and skills required for proficiency. It is important to ensure that the competencies are measurable and observable, and that they align with the organization's values and goals.

5: Develop a Competency Model

The final step is to develop a competency model, which is a visual representation of the competencies required for success in the identified roles or functions. The competency model can take various forms, such as a matrix or a wheel, and should clearly illustrate the relationship between the competencies and the roles or functions.

Considerations

Building a competency model requires careful consideration and planning.

Here are some additional considerations to keep in mind:
• Involve stakeholders: It is important to involve stakeholders, such as managers and employees, in the development of the competency model to ensure buy-in and alignment with organizational goals.
• Keep it simple: Competency models should be clear and concise, with a focus on the most critical competencies required for success.
• Continuously review and update: Competency models should be reviewed and updated regularly to ensure they remain relevant and effective.
• Use the competency model: The competency model should be used in all relevant HR processes, such as recruitment, performance management, and training and development.

Building a competency model is an important process for organizations to define the skills, behaviours, and knowledge required for success in a particular role or within the company as a whole. By following the key steps and considerations outlined in this blog post, organizations can develop effective competency models that drive performance and success.

4.2 Profiling Competency Framework for a Particular Role

To identify the role-specific skills required for enhanced performance. Industry specific functional and behavioural competencies which need to be developed for enhanced performance. The approach to developing a competency framework for a particular role is as follows:

1. Understand the organizational structure and environmental variables in the strategic business context.

2. Detail role descriptions for positions. Defining and scaling (relative importance and mastery level) of specific behaviours for each identified competency as a measure of performance.

3. Develop a competency framework considering the core values and culture of the organization in addition to specific functional and level requirements. This should be consistent with the company's vision and mission.

4. Validate the competency framework through a workshop, which should include functional experts and top management personnel to define critical and desirable competencies. And also, to substantiate the extent to which competencies differentiate between high and average performers by validating the content and criteria.

Note: The competency framework includes technical competencies, behavioural competencies, and proficiency levels. It is important to specify behavioural indicators that allow observation and assessment of each competency.

4.3 Potential Assessment Centre for Competency Mapping

A comprehensive understanding of competencies and roles is achieved through a competency mapping exercise. This is done through which the most critical success driving behaviours for specific roles are established.

Against the validated competency framework, an individual's potential is identified through an assessment Centre process outlined below:

1. Design Assessment Centre

2. Conduct an Assessment Centre

3. Map individual competencies and gaps

4. Finally assess organizational capability and gaps.

A link between people and competencies is established through an effective system of measuring an individual's proficiency on the desired competencies for the role. The link between people and roles is established through effective measuring tools that evaluate the person's performance in the role. On-the-job performance of an individual is evaluated using a performance management system.

The Assessment Centre is a powerful tool in management's hands for selection and development. It can be used for management promotions, fast track schemes, high potential lists, and job changes. As a development tool, it helps with succession planning, identifying training needs and career development.

Developing and conducting an Assessment Centre should follow basic principles in terms of accuracy, fairness, reliability, legality, efficiency, multiple assessors, multiple tests, and optimal stress levels. It would involve two types of exercise, i.e., group exercises and individual exercises.

Group exercises

For potential assessment, the following group exercises are conducted:

1. Assigned Role Exercises: Used to assess negotiating skills, decision-making skills, and risk-taking skills;

2. Unassigned Role Exercises: Used to assess uncertainty handling, change orientation, ethical behaviour and global orientation; and

3. Team Exercises: Used to assess teamwork and solve problems efficiently

Individual exercises

For potential assessment, the following individual exercises are conducted:

1. In-Basket Exercises: Used to assess planning, organizing, deciding, managing delegate;

2. Learning skill Inventory/Psychometric Inventories: Used to assess learning ability, leverage knowledge and indicate behavioural patterns; and

3. Interpersonal Effectiveness Module: Used to assess interpersonal effectiveness excommunication skills, patience and interpersonal skills

Inputs for analysis of an individual's potential and behavioural patterns are also collected through multilateral feedback (self, peer, subordinate, customer and superior assessment), behavioural event interviews, career aspiration interviews, career history, etc. In order to minimize assessors' bias and ensure objectivity and uniformity multiple trained assessors are used for each competency assessment.

The competencies gaps can be found out by comparing the desired competency (proficiency) levels and displayed competency levels as indicated in Figure 4.1.

Based on the above exercises, feedback details for individuals on their strengths and developmental areas are prepared.

Competencies with positive gaps indicate areas of improvement; those with negative gaps indicate strengths.

The gap areas need to be analyzed and prioritized based on their importance. There are gaps that need to be filled on an individual, departmental, and organizational level. To accomplish this, milestones are agreed upon for each individual in terms of projects, job rotations, transfers, training, and enrichment. In HR, establishing a Development Monitoring Cell will help create a project plan that includes deadlines and escalation options. Additionally, it would have a feedback system for employees and bosses to provide feedback. An organization's strengths and weaknesses are determined by its average assessment results.

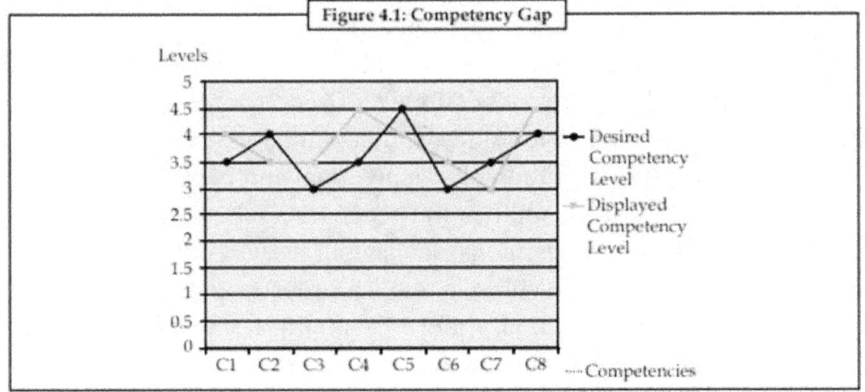

Enter Caption

4.4 Methods of Competency Mapping

Competency mapping is the process of identifying and assessing the skills, knowledge, abilities, and behaviours required for success in a particular job or role. Here are some common methods of competency mapping:

1. Job analysis: This involves analyzing the job requirements and identifying the competencies needed to perform the job effectively.

2. Behavioural event interviews: This is a structured interview technique that focuses on specific events or situations in which the candidate demonstrated the required competencies.

3. Self-assessment: This involves having employees assess their own competencies and identifying areas for improvement.

4. 360-degree feedback: This involves soliciting feedback from multiple sources, including supervisors, peers, subordinates, and customers, to gain a comprehensive understanding of an employee's competencies.

5. Assessment canters: This involves a series of exercises and simulations that assess an employee's competencies in a variety of situations.

6. Performance appraisal: This involves evaluating an employee's performance against specific job competencies.

7. Competency frameworks: This is a structured approach that defines the competencies required for success in a particular job or role and provides a framework for assessing and developing these competencies.

By using one or a combination of these methods, organizations can develop a better understanding of their employees' competencies and identify areas for improvement in order to enhance individual and organizational performance.

Basically, it is not easy to identify all the competencies required to fulfill the job requirement. However, a number of methods and approaches have been developed and successfully tried out in the organization. These methods have helped managers identify and reinforce and/or develop these competencies. This is both for the individual's growth and the growth of our organization.

1. The 360-degree multi-rating is a method of objectively assessing employees' performance. This appraisal method takes care of many things like what kind of behaviour a person has with superiors, subordinates, peers etc.

2. In organizational surveys, employees rate themselves after the questionnaire is filled out. Questionnaires are written lists of questions that users fill out and then return. The techniques are used at various stages of development, depending on the questions asked in the questionnaires.

3. Assessment centre: An assessment centre identifies growth potential. It is a method (not a location) that uses a variety of techniques to evaluate employees for the purpose of manpower and decisions. An essential feature of the assessment centre used by our organization is the use of situational tests to observe specific job behaviour. Since it is pertaining to a job, elements related to the job are simulated through a variety of tests. The assessors observe behaviour and evaluate what they have observed. This results in identifying the strengths and weaknesses of the attributes being studied.

4. With job analysis tools, companies can extract core competencies from within their own organization and have experts rate any job title or position according to a standard competency scale. The accumulated ratings are converted into a composite template defining the ideal competency set. An employee or job applicant completes a self-report, which is mapped against a template. Therefore, skill or competency gaps are identified and training decisions are based on them.

Task: Develop a competency mapping questionnaire

4.5 Summary

• Competency Mapping begins with identifying key competencies for an organization and/or a job and incorporating those competencies throughout the various processes (i.e., job Organizational evaluation, training, and recruitment.

• The link between people and competencies is established through effective measures of an individual's proficiency on the desired competencies.

• Competencies are a broad term referring to an individual's demonstrated knowledge, skills, behaviours, experience, life view and values. They constitute observable, behavioural acts that require a combination of all these attributes to execute.

• Competency mappings serve as behaviour-based standards of performance against which people and organizations can be measured over time.

4.6 Keywords

a) Assessment centre: An assessment centre is a mechanism to identify growth potential. It is a method (not a location) that uses a variety of techniques to evaluate employees for the purpose of human resources and decisions.

b) Behavioural Indicators: Behavioural indicators describe behaviours, thought patterns, abilities and traits that contribute to superior performance.

c) Competency: Skills and abilities described in behavioural terms that are coachable, observable, measurable and critical to a successful individual's or organization's performance.

4.7 Self-Assessment
Fill in the blanks:

1. The competencies of the respective job description also become factors for assessment on ....

2. Exceptional competencies of high performers are set as .... for evaluating competency levels of employees.

3. The .... is a powerful tool in the hands of the management for selection and development.

4. .... between desired and displayed competencies indicate areas of improvement.

State whether the following statements are true or false:

5. Assessment centre is a mechanism to identify growth potential.

6. Acquired competencies can be found by comparing the desired competencies (proficiency) levels and displayed competency levels.

7. Average assessment results identify strengths and gaps in an organization's capabilities.

8. On-the-job performance of the individual is evaluated based on a performance planning.

9. The competency framework includes technical competencies and behavioural competencies and the proficiency levels required for each competency.

Answers: Self-Assessment

1. performance evaluation 2. standards

3. Assessment Centre 4. Positive gaps

5. True 6. True

7. True 8. False

9. True

4.8 Review Questions

1. "A characteristic is not a competency unless it predicts something meaningful in the real World". Discuss.

2. "Competency mapping forms an excellent tool for optimizing human capital"

Elucidate.

3. A job analysis tool helps companies uncover key competencies from their internal experts. The company can have any number of rating experts contribute ratings. Examine the differences between job analysis and other competency mapping approaches.

4. "A link between people and competencies is established through an effective system of measuring an individual's proficiency on the desired competencies for the role. "Discuss.

5. Make a graphic representation showing the comparison between the desired competency level and the displayed competency level.

6. Assigned role exercises are group exercises used to assess negotiating, decision making, and risk-taking skills. Suggest some other individual and group exercises used for potential assessment.

7. Construct a sample competency assessment questionnaire.

8. "The competencies of the respective job description also become factors for assessment on performance evaluation." Discuss.

9. What is the role of an assessment centre as a development tool?

10. Develop a competency framework for a particular role.

CHAPTER FIVE

Performance Appraisal

Objectives

The following can be accomplished after studying this unit:
• Describe the performance appraisal process
• Explain the approaches to performance appraisal

Introduction

Performance appraisal is a systematic and formal process that evaluates an employee's job performance and productivity over a specific period. It is an essential aspect of human resource management that provides feedback to employees about their strengths and weaknesses, helps identify areas for improvement, and facilitates career development.

The performance appraisal process involves setting performance expectations, measuring actual performance against those expectations, providing feedback to employees, and setting goals for future performance. It can be conducted through various methods such as self-appraisals, supervisor appraisals, 360-degree feedback, and peer reviews.

The objective of performance appraisal is to identify areas where an employee can improve their performance and to provide feedback to help them grow and develop in their role. It also serves as a basis for making decisions related to promotions, transfers, salary increases, and terminations.

Effective performance appraisal can lead to increased employee motivation and engagement, higher job satisfaction, and improved organizational performance. However, poorly designed or implemented performance appraisal processes can lead to demotivation, employee dissatisfaction, and even legal issues.

In some organizations, appraisal systems are perceived as causing more problems than they are solving. The experience of the past few decades has shown that appraisal is not a gimmick. Employee morale and trust climate can be negatively affected by appraisals if they are not handled properly.

In general, performance appraisal is an essential tool for managing employee performance and facilitating employee development and growth within an organization.

5.1 Meaning of Performance Appraisal

Performance appraisal, also known as performance evaluation or performance review, is a systematic and formal process of assessing an employee's job performance and productivity over a specific period. It involves setting performance expectations, measuring actual performance against those expectations, providing feedback to employees, and setting goals for future performance.

The primary objective of performance appraisal is to evaluate an employee's job performance and provide feedback on their strengths and weaknesses. It serves as a tool for managing employee performance, identifying areas for improvement, and facilitating employee development and growth.

Performance appraisal can be conducted using various methods such as self-appraisals, supervisor appraisals, 360-degree feedback, and peer reviews. The appraisal process can be carried out periodically, such as annually or bi-annually, or as needed.

The outcomes of performance appraisal can be used to make decisions related to promotions, transfers, salary increases, and training and development opportunities. It also helps to align employee performance with the overall goals and objectives of the organization.

Effective performance appraisal can lead to increased employee motivation and engagement, higher job satisfaction, and improved organizational performance. However, poorly designed or implemented performance appraisal processes can lead to demotivation, employee dissatisfaction, and even legal issues.

5.2 Process of Performance Appraisal

The process of performance appraisal typically involves the following steps:

a) Setting Performance Expectations: The first step in the performance appraisal process is to set performance expectations and goals for the employee. This involves defining the key performance indicators (KPIs) that the employee should focus on and aligning their goals with the objectives of the organization.

b) Performance Measurement: Once the performance expectations are set, the employee's performance is measured against those expectations. This can be done through various methods, such as self-appraisal, supervisor appraisal, peer review, or 360-degree feedback.

c) Feedback: After measuring the employee's performance, feedback is provided to the employee regarding their strengths and areas for improvement. The feedback can be positive or negative, and it should be constructive and specific.

d) Goal Setting: Based on the feedback provided, goals are set for the employee to improve their performance. These goals should be specific, measurable, achievable, relevant, and time-bound (SMART).

e) Performance Review: The performance appraisal process culminates in a performance review meeting between the employee and their supervisor or manager. During this meeting, the employee's performance is discussed, feedback is provided, and goals for the future are established.

f) Follow-up: After the performance review, the employee's progress is monitored, and they are given support and guidance to achieve their goals. This involves regular check-ins and communication between the employee and their supervisor.

The performance appraisal process is ongoing and should be conducted regularly to provide employees with feedback, improve their performance, and help them achieve their career goals. It is essential to ensure that the process is fair, objective, and transparent to maintain employee morale and engagement.

Thus, meaningful performance appraisals benefit both the employee and manager. The appraisal is a time for employees to learn how their managers rate their performance. Managers can find out how employees perceive their performance in a formal appraisal interview. Planning an appraisal strategy involves:

Prior to the appraisal

1. Establish key task areas and performance goals.
2. Set performance goals for each key task area.
3. Get the facts.
4. Schedule each appraisal interview well in advance.

At the time of appraisal

1. Encourage two-way communication.
2. Discuss and agree on future performance goals.
3. Think about how you can help employees to achieve more at work.

4. Record notes from the interview.

5. End the interview on an upbeat note.

   A few days after the appraisal

1. Prepare a formal record of the interview.

2. Monitor performance.

3. Feedback session – tell and sell, tell and listen, problem solving.

4. Developing a need-based training program.

5. Working out reward-based incentives

5.3 Approaches of Performance Appraisal

There are several approaches to performance appraisal, including:

a) Trait-Based Approach: This approach focuses on evaluating an employee's personality traits, such as their attitude, initiative, and teamwork skills. The appraisal is based on the supervisor's subjective judgment of the employee's traits.

b) Behavioural-Based Approach: This approach focuses on evaluating an employee's observable behaviours, such as their punctuality, communication skills, and problem-solving ability. The appraisal is based on specific examples of the employee's behaviour.

c) Results-Based Approach: This approach focuses on evaluating an employee's results or outcomes, such as their sales figures, customer satisfaction ratings, or project completion rates. The appraisal is based on objective measures of the employee's performance.

d) Competency-Based Approach: This approach focuses on evaluating an employee's competencies, such as their knowledge, skills, and abilities. The appraisal is based on how well the employee demonstrates these competencies in their job.

e) 360-Degree Feedback Approach: This approach involves gathering feedback from multiple sources, such as the employee's supervisor, peers, subordinates, and customers. The appraisal is based on the combined feedback from these sources.

f) Continuous Performance Management Approach: This approach involves providing continuous feedback and coaching to employees throughout the year, rather than conducting a formal appraisal once or twice a year.

Each approach has its advantages and disadvantages, and organizations may choose to use a combination of approaches to evaluate employee performance. It is essential to select the approach that best aligns with the organization's goals and objectives and ensures that the performance appraisal process is fair, transparent, and objective.

George Odiorne has identified four basic performance appraisal approaches.

1. Personality-based systems: In such systems the appraisal form consists of a list of personality traits that presumably are significant in the jobs of the individuals being appraised. Such traits as initiative, drive, intelligence, ingenuity, creativity, loyalty and trustworthiness appear on most lists.

2. Generalized descriptive systems: Similar to personality-based systems, they differ in the type of descriptive term used. Often, they include the qualities or actions of presumably good managers: "organizes, plans, controls, motivates others, delegates, communicates, makes things happen," and so on. Such a system, like the personality-based system, might be useful if meticulous care was taken to define the meaning of each term in respect to actual results.

3. Behavioural descriptive systems: Such systems feature detailed job analysis and job descriptions, including specific statements of the actual behaviour required of successful employees.

4. Result-centered systems: These appraisal systems (sometimes called work-centered or job-centered systems) are directly job related.

They require that managers and subordinates sit down at the start of each work evaluation period and determine the work to be done in all areas of responsibility and functions, and the specific standards of performance to be used in each area.

When introducing performance appraisal, a job description in the form of a questionnaire must be preferred. A typical questionnaire addressed to an individual would cover the following points:

1. What is your job title?

2. To whom are you responsible?

3. Who is responsible for you?

4. What is your main purpose and what are your main areas of responsibility?

5. What is the size of your job in output or sales targets, number of items processed, number of people managed, number of customers? What targets or performance standards have been assigned to your job? Are there any other ways to measure the effectiveness with which you do your job?

6. Is there other information about your job?

Case Study: TCS Asks 1,300 Employees to Leave

Around 1,300 employees of Tata Consultancy Services will resign from the company following a routine bi-annual performance appraisal. The employees being asked to leave will constitute around one per cent of the total staff, numbering over 1,30,000, said a spokesperson for the company. Their leaving the company is not part of any cost-cutting exercise designed to cope with the economic slowdown, she said. TCS' bi-annual performance appraisal throws up underperformers who are given special training; but if they are not up to the mark in the next appraisal, they are asked to leave

Last year, the company had asked 500 employees to leave following such an appraisal. Analysts held that although the staff cut was for under-performance, it is possible that in times of slowdown companies might come up with more stringent standards for performance.

TCS' current utilisation rate (the proportion of staff working on projects) is 75 per cent, said the spokesperson. This does not mean that 25 per cent are benched, for the rest consist of administrative and other staff who are not directly on projects, she said.

Source: www.thehindubusinessline.com

Task: Describe the key elements of performance appraisal.

5.4 Summary

- Performance appraisal is a systematic and formal process that evaluates an employee's job performance and productivity over a specific period. It involves setting performance expectations, measuring actual performance against those expectations, providing feedback to employees, and setting goals for future performance. The process can be conducted through various methods such as self-appraisals, supervisor appraisals, 360-degree feedback, and peer reviews.

- The objective of performance appraisal is to identify areas where an employee can improve their performance and to provide feedback to help them grow and develop in their role. Effective performance appraisal can lead to increased employee motivation and engagement, higher job satisfaction, and improved organizational performance.

- There are several approaches to performance appraisal, including trait-based, behavioural-based, results-based, competency-based, 360-degree feedback, and continuous performance management. Organizations may choose to use a combination of approaches to evaluate employee performance.

- It is a process of estimating or judging the value, excellent qualities or status of a person or thing. It is a process of collecting, analyzing, and evaluating data relative to job behaviour and results of individuals. The appraisal system is organized on the principle of goals and management by objectives.
- Performance appraisals can be formal or informal. Formal appraisals are former systems that schedule regular sessions to discuss employee performance. Informal appraisals are unplanned, often just chance statements made in passing about an employee's performance.
- The main difference between performance management and appraisal systems is their respective emphasis and spirit. Good organizations in the past have used performance appraisal systems as performance management systems.
- Performance appraisal plans are designed to meet the needs of the organization and the individual. It is increasingly viewed as central to good human resource management.
- Organizations use performance appraisals for three purposes: administrative, employee development and programme assessment. Programme appraisal commonly serves an administrative purpose by providing employers with a rational for making many personnel decisions. This includes decisions relating to pay increases, promotions, demotions, terminations and transfers.
- There are two types of performance appraisal systems normally used in organizations: (i) close ended appraisal system and, (ii) open ended appraisal system.
- Generally, performance appraisal is an essential tool for managing employee performance and facilitating employee development and growth within an organization. It helps align employee performance with the overall goals and objectives of the organization, which can lead to increased productivity and profitability.

5.5 Keywords

- Close Ended Appraisal System: In this, a confidential report is submitted on the employee's performance.

- MBO: It involves the setting out clearly defi ne goals of an employee in agreement with his superior.

- Open Ended Appraisal System: In this, the individual's performance is discussed with him, and he is ranked on a five- or ten-point rating scale.

- Performance Appraisal: It is a systematic evaluation of the present and potential capabilities of personnel and employees by their superiors, superior's or a professional form outside.

- Self-Appraisal: It gives a chance to the employee to look at his/her strengths and weaknesses, his achievements, and judge his own performance.

5.6 Self-Assessment
Fill in the blanks:

1. .... appraisals are unplanned as they include just statements being made about employee performance.

2. Performance appraisal undertaken for .... gives employees complete feedback on their performance.

3. Performance of an individual employee is monitored .... the appraisal process.

4. Work-centered appraisal systems are directly .... related.

5. In a .... appraisal, the performance of the employees is not disclosed.

6. Performance appraisal is a systematic evaluation of the present .... of personnel and employees by their superiors, superior's or a professional form outside.

7. Organizations need to measure employee performance to determine whether acceptable .... of performance are maintained.

8. A meaningful performance appraisal is a .... process that benefits both the employee and the manager.

9. .... systems feature detailed job analysis and job descriptions, including specific statements of the actual behavior required from successfully employees.

10. When introducing performance appraisal, a job description in the form of a .... has to be preferred.

Answers: Self-Assessment

1. Informal 2. employee development

3. after 4. job

5. open ended 6. potential capabilities

7. standards 8. two-way

9. Behavioural descriptive 10. questionnaire

5.7 Review Questions

1. "Many people believe that appraisal systems have created more problems than they have solved". Discuss.

2. "Performance appraisal is increasingly viewed as central to good human resource management." Substantiate.

3. George Odiorne has identified four basic performance appraisal approaches. Explain them.

4. What is the meaning of the statement that "Differences in perception and value systems Influence evaluations"?

5. Is appraising potential is more difficult than appraising performance?

6. "A meaningful performance appraisal is a two-way process that benefits both the employee and the manager." Discuss.

7. Performance appraisals can be formal or informal. Evaluate both formal and informal performance appraisal systems.

8. How will you evaluate performance value?

9. Design a questionnaire to evaluate an individual's performance.

10. Design a performance appraisal strategy to evaluate manager performance

Methods of Performance Appraisal

Objectives

Studying this chapter will enable you to do the following:

• Analyze performance appraisal methods

• Identify common errors when rating

Introduction

Performance appraisal is a formal system used by organizations to evaluate the performance of their employees. It involves assessing an employee's job performance against predetermined goals, objectives, and standards. Performance appraisal is used to provide feedback to employees about their performance, identify areas for improvement, and recognize high performers.

There are several methods used in performance appraisal, each with its own advantages and disadvantages. Some common methods of performance appraisal include:

• Graphic Rating Scales: This is a method where an employee is evaluated based on a set of pre-determined performance criteria such as job knowledge, quality of work, communication skills, and attendance. The employee is rated on a scale, and the final score determines their performance.

• Behavioural Observation Scale: This method involves evaluating an employee's behaviour on a set of pre-determined dimensions such as communication, leadership, teamwork, and problem-solving skills. The evaluator observes the employee's behaviour and rates them on a scale.

• 360-Degree Feedback: This method involves feedback from multiple sources, including the employee, their manager, peers, and subordinates. The feedback is used to provide a comprehensive evaluation of an employee's performance.

• Management by Objectives: This method involves setting specific, measurable, achievable, relevant, and time-bound (SMART) objectives for an employee. The employee's performance is evaluated based on how well they achieve these objectives.

• Critical Incident Method: This method involves documenting critical incidents where an employee's performance either exceeded or fell short of expectations. The incidents are then used to evaluate the employee's overall performance.

Each of these methods has its advantages and disadvantages. The choice of the method used depends on the organization's culture, objectives, and goals.

There are three types of performance appraisal, according to Structure and Sayles: traditional performance ratings, new-rating methods, and result-oriented appraisals. Each is described as follows:

6.1 Traditional Performance Rating

Traditional rating involves the immediate supervisor of the individual being evaluated. In some cases, attempts are made to accomplish the rating by a committee consisting of the immediate supervisor, the supervisor's superior and one or two more officers of the company who are familiar with the ratings. Ratings by the committee bring several viewpoints together and overcome superior bias, they take a lot of time. The conventional rating scale form incorporates several factors, such as job knowledge, judgment, organizing ability, dependability, creativity, dealing with people, delegation, and leadership. The rating is assigned by putting a tick mark horizontally. Descriptive phrases are often given to guide the appraiser while evaluating the rates. This method is very simple to understand and apply. Ratings on specific factors can identify areas in which the individual requires further development. The ratings on specific factors can be summated to obtain a composite performance score

The merit-rating scales are frequently criticized from the standpoints of clarity in standards, differing perceptions, excessive leniency or strictness, the central tendency, the halo effect, and the impact of an individual's job. The basic criticism of traditional performance rating is concerned with its emphasis on personality traits instead of job performance. Such rating is highly subjective without objective standards.

The traditional performance rating method is one of the oldest and most widely used methods of performance appraisal. It involves evaluating an employee's performance based on a predetermined set of criteria, which typically include job knowledge, quality of work, productivity, communication skills, and teamwork.

In this method, the employee is rated on a scale, typically ranging from 1 to 5, with 1 being the lowest rating and 5 being the highest. The rating scale may also include intermediate levels, such as 2, 3, and 4.

The traditional performance rating method usually involves an annual or bi-annual review process, where the employee's supervisor or manager evaluates their performance and provides feedback. The feedback is then used to determine the employee's rating, which can be used to make decisions about promotions, bonuses, and salary increases.

One of the advantages of the traditional performance rating method is that it provides a clear and objective way of evaluating employee performance. It also allows for easy comparison between employees, which can be useful for making decisions about promotions or salary increases.

However, there are also several disadvantages to this method. One of the main criticisms of the traditional performance rating method is that it can be too subjective, with different supervisors or managers having different standards for evaluation. This can lead to inconsistent and unfair evaluations.

Additionally, the traditional performance rating method can be demotivating for employees, especially if they receive a low rating. This can lead to a focus on short-term performance rather than long-term development and improvement.

In general, the traditional performance rating method remains a widely used method of performance appraisal, but many organizations are also exploring alternative methods that address some of the limitations of this approach.

6.2 New rating methods

Because of several inadequacies in the traditional rating scale, attempts have been made to devise new procedures less susceptible to the above weaknesses. Among these include rank order, paired comparison, forced distribution forced choice, critical incident and field review. These methods are discussed below.

1. Rank-order Procedure: It is effective where ten or a lesser number of individuals are to be evaluated. According to this procedure, each individual is assigned a rank such as first, second, third and so on. If the evaluation process involves several traits, the ranking is made separately for each

trait. Although this method is simple to understand and easy to apply, it becomes cumbersome and difficult when large numbers of employees are to be evaluated in an organization.

2. Paired-comparison System: Under this, each individual is compared with everyone else. The appraiser is required to tick the name of the individual he considers to be the best performer for the trait in question. The final ranking is determined by how often he is judged better than his counterpart. This method becomes complicated when the number of people being evaluated is large.

3. Forced Distribution Procedure: It is a form of comparative evaluation in which an evaluator rates subordinates according to a specified distribution. Here judgments are made on a relative basis i.e., a person is assessed relative to his performance in the group he works in. This procedure can be used for numerous traits if required by evaluating individuals separately for each trait. The forced distribution method eliminates rating errors such as leniency and central tendency.

4. Forced Choice Technique: It forces the appraiser to select from a series of several statements or traits, the one which best fits the individual and the one which least fits, and each of these statements is assigned a score. Since the appraiser does not know the score value of statements, this method prevents the appraiser from deliberately checking only the most favorable traits. Moreover, the appraiser cannot introduce personal bias into the evaluation process because he does not know which statement is indicative of effective performance. This enhances the overall objectivity of this procedure.

5. Critical Incident Method: This technique of performance appraisal was developed by Flanagan and Burns. Under this procedure, attempts are made to devise for each job a list of critical job requirements. Superiors are trained to look out for critical incidents on the part of subordinates in accomplishing job requirements. The superiors note the incidents as they happen and, in the process, build up a record of each subordinate with debit on the minus side and credit on the plus side. This procedure is based on objective evidence instead of subjective ratings.

6. Field Review: It is an appraisal by someone outside the employee's own department, usually someone from the corporate office or from the employee's own human resources department. The field review process involves review of employee records, an interview with the employee, and sometimes with the employee Field review as an appraisal method is used

primary in making promotion decisions at the managerial level. Field reviews are also useful when comparable information is needed from employees in different units or locations.

6.3 Results-oriented Appraisal

Results-oriented appraisals are based on concrete performance targets established jointly between the supervisor and the subordinate. This procedure is known as Management by Objectives (MBO).

MBO is, essentially, a method of mutual goal-setting, measuring progress towards goals, taking action to assure attainment, feedback, and participation. It is a result-oriented philosophy, enabling employees to measure progress toward a goal they often helped to set. In the goals-setting phase of MBO, a superior and subordinate discuss job performance problems and a goal is agreed upon. Along with mutual goal-setting, a major component of MBO is the performance review session between the superior and subordinate, which takes place regularly to evaluate progress towards specified goals.

The key features of management by objectives are as follows:

1. Superior and subordinate get together and jointly agree on the list of the principal duties and areas of responsibility for the individual's job.

2. In collaboration with his superior, the subordinate sets his own short-term performance goals.

3. They agree upon criteria for measuring and evaluating performance.

4. From time to time, as decided upon, the superior and subordinate meet to evaluate progress towards the agreed-upon goals. At those meetings, revised or modified goals are set for the ensuing period.

5. The superior plays a supportive role. He tries, on an ongoing basis, to help the subordinate achieve the agreed-upon goals. He counsels and coaches.

6. In the appraisal process, the superior plays less of the role of a judge and more of the role of one who helps the subordinate attain the organization's goals or targets.

7. The process focuses on results achieved rather than personal traits.

Did you know? What is MBO?

MBO stands for Management by Objectives, which is a method of performance appraisal that involves setting specific, measurable, achievable, relevant, and time-bound (SMART) objectives for employees. This method was first developed by management theorist Peter Drucker in the 1950s.

In the MBO method, employees work with their supervisors or managers to establish clear and specific goals for their performance. These goals are aligned with the overall objectives of the organization and are designed to be challenging but achievable. The goals are then monitored and evaluated throughout the year, with regular feedback provided to employees on their progress.

One of the key advantages of the MBO method is that it focuses on setting clear and measurable goals for employee performance, which can help to align individual goals with the overall objectives of the organization. It also provides a structured process for evaluating employee performance and providing feedback.

Another advantage of the MBO method is that it can be motivating for employees, as they are involved in the process of setting their own goals and are held accountable for achieving them. This can help to create a sense of ownership and responsibility for their work.

However, there are also some potential drawbacks to the MBO method. For example, setting overly ambitious goals can lead to stress and burnout, while setting goals that are too easy can lead to complacency. Additionally, the MBO method may not be suitable for all types of jobs, such as those that require more creativity or flexibility.

Generally, the MBO method is a widely used approach to performance appraisal that can be effective in aligning individual goals with organizational objectives and motivating employees to achieve their best performance.

The definition of MBO, as expressed by its foremost proponent, Dr. George S. Odiorne, is: "Management by objectives is a process whereby the superior and subordinate managers of an organization jointly identify its common goals, define each individual's major areas of responsibility in terms of the results expected of him, and use these measures as guides for operating the unit and assessing the contribution of each of its members."

MBO as a mutual goal setting exercise is most appropriate for technical, professional, supervisory and executive personnel. In these positions, there is generally enough latitude and room for discretion. This makes it possible for the person to set work goals, tackling various projects, and discovering more creative ways to solve problems. This method is generally not applied to lower categories of workers because their jobs are usually too restricted in scope. There is not much discretionary opportunity to shape their jobs. MBO may be viewed as a management system rather than an appraisal method. Successful implementation of MBO requires written mission statements that are prepared at the highest levels of top management. Mission statements provide the coherence necessary to make top-down and bottom-up goal setting become sensible and compatible. MBO can be applied successfully to an organization with sufficient autonomy, personnel, budget allocation, and policy integrity. Managers are expected to perform so that organization goals are achieved. Too often MBO is installed topdown in a dictatorial manner with a little or no accompanying training. If properly implemented, it serves as a powerful and useful tool for managerial performance.

MBO is a tool inextricably connected to team building. This is so that team members' work commitment can be increased and their desire to excel can be inspired. It is imperative to have effective teamwork among managers or subordinates. The group of employees or subordinates must be considered a team that needs to be brought together. Goals should be set by managers-subordinate pairs, and teams. The basic superior-subordinate relationship in an organization is not undermined by this concept of team goal setting. Lines of responsibility, authority, and accountability remain clear.

MBO has many advantages, since it:
1. Providing a way of measuring objectively subordinate performance.
2. Co-ordinates individual performance with company goals.
3. Establishes the job to be done and outlines job accomplishment expectations.
4. Improves the superior-subordinate relationship through regular communication.
5. Foster increased competence, personal growth, and career opportunity.
6. Aids in the development of a comprehensive planning system.
7. It provides a basis for more equitable salary determinations, especially incentive bonuses.
8. Develops factual data for promotion criteria.
9. Stimulates self-motivation, self-discipline and self-control.
10. Serves as a device for management functions integration

MBO has certain potential drawbacks, such as:
1. It often lacks top management support and commitment.
2. Its objectives are often difficult to establish.
3. Its implementation creates excessive paperwork if not closely monitored.
4. It concentrates too much on the short run at the expense of long-range

planning.

5. There is a possibility that it will take too much time.

Note: Steps in MBO

MBO has four main steps:

1. Defining the job: Review, with the subordinates, his or her key responsibilities and duties.

2. Set objectives (define expected results): Show in measurable terms what the person is expected to accomplish.

3. Measure the results: compare actual goals achieved with expected results.

4. Provide feedback, appraise: Hold periodic performance review meetings with subordinates to discuss and evaluate their progress in achieving expected results.

6.4 360-degree Feedback or 360-degree Appraisal

Traditionally, in most performance evaluations a supervisor evaluates the performance of a subordinate. Recently, an innovative approach has been enunciated by western management gurus, which is known as 360-degree appraisal - performance management system in which people receive performance feedback from those on all sides of them in the organization.

360-degree respondents for an employee can be his/her peers, managers (i.e., superiors), subordinates, team members, customers, suppliers/ vendors – anyone who comes into contact with the employee and can provide valuable insights and information or feedback regarding the employee's "on-the-job" performance.

Did you know? 360-degree feedback is also known as 'multi-ratter feedback', as it is the most comprehensive appraisal where feedback about employees' performance comes from all the sources that come into contact with the employee on his job.

360-degree appraisal has four integral components:

1. Self-appraisal

2. Superior's appraisal

3. Subordinates' appraisal

4. Peer appraisal.

Self-appraisal gives employees a chance to look at their strengths and weaknesses, his achievements, and judge his own performance. Employees' responsibilities and actual performance are assessed by their superiors in the traditional 360-degree performance appraisal.

In evaluating a subordinate, a supervisor is able to evaluate the employee on the basis of a variety of criteria, including communication and motivating abilities, the superior's delegation skills, and leadership abilities. Also known as internal customers, the correct feedback given by peers can help to find employees' abilities to work in a team, co-operation and sensitivity towards others.

As self-assessment is an essential component of 360-degree performance appraisals, these appraisals have a high level of employee involvement and have the greatest impact on behaviour and performance of employees. It provides a "360-degree review" of employees' performance and is considered one of the most credible performance appraisal methods.

360-degree performance appraisal is also a powerful developmental tool because when conducted at regular intervals (say yearly) it helps to keep track of changes others' perceptions about employees. A 360-degree appraisal is generally more appropriate for managers as it helps assess their leadership and management styles. This technique is effectively used across the globe for performance appraisals. Some of the Indian organizations following it are Wipro, Infosys, and Reliance Industries etc.

American companies use 360-degree feedback. Companies that practice 360-degree appraisals include Motorola, Semco Brazil, British Petroleum, British Airways, Central Television, etc. Barring a few multinational companies, in India this appraisal system is uncommon.

This form of performance evaluation can be very beneficial to managers because it typically gives them a much wider range of performance-related feedback than a traditional evaluation. That is, rather than focusing narrowly on objective performance, such as sales increases or productivity gains, 360-degree often focuses on interpersonal relations and style. Of course, to benefit from 360-degree feedback, a manager must have thick skin. The manager is likely to hear some personal comments on sensitive topics, which may be threatening. 360-degree feedback systems must be carefully managed to focus on constructive rather than destructive criticism.

Advantages of 360-degree Appraisal
For Employees
1. Can uncover hidden lights and blind spots.
2. Feedback coming from a number of different people is more likely to be accepted.
3. Helps individuals gain a realistic view of how others perceive them.
4. Inspires people to take ownership of their own learning and development.
5. Provides feedback in quantifiable form on a structured range of

behaviours.

For the Team

1. It helps people understand how their behaviour influences both their own personal effectiveness and the smooth running of an organization.
2. Supports teamwork by involving team members in development.
3. Increased communication between team members.
4. Higher levels of trust and better communication as individuals identify breakdown causes.
5. Increased team effectiveness.

For the Organization

1. Better career development planning and implementation for employees.
2. Improve customer service by having customers contribute to evaluation.
3. Reinforced corporate culture by linking survey items to organizational leadership competencies and company values.
4. Helps with training needs analysis.

The pitfalls of 360-degree Feedback

1. An action plan that ensures transparent and clear implementation of appraisals with employee accountability.
2. Effective follow-up is the prime requirement for 360-degree feedback. Failure to follow-up may harm more than benefit.
3. 360-degree feedback is a time-consuming and expensive assessment process. Without adequate resources to implement the process, it will go nowhere and impose a financial burden on the organisation.
4. The trust and confidence of employees who undergo this feedback assessment process determine its outcome. There are many people who view this appraisal as a tool for downsizing.
5. The process involves a lot of paperwork.
6. During the feedback assessment, both management and employees have a high chance of being subjective.
7. Many times the confidentiality of the appraisal cannot be ensured by the HR department.
8. Since the assessment is based on qualitative data, it may not be possible to ensure unambiguous, clear, specific and observable and quantifiable formats.

Did you know? In what ways does 360-degree feedback add value?

360-degree feedback enables an organization to focus on developmental efforts, at the individual and group level, in the present business environment where the company's success depends on continuous revolution, which is possible through organizational development. 360-degree feedback facilitates individual capabilities and behaviours alignment with organizational strategies. It adds value to the organization in different ways:

1. 360-degree feedback provides a better understanding of individuals' work performance.

2. 360-degree feedback provides a multifaceted view of employees from different sources.

3. 360-degree feedback provides a better understanding of employees' developmental needs.

4. By giving 360-degree feedback, one can gain a deeper understanding of their role expectations.

5. 360-degree feedback provides increased understanding of competence and competency in various roles.

6. 360-degree feedback enhances morale among those who perform and contribute well to the organization.

7. 360-degree feedback reduces training costs by identifying common development needs.

8. 360-degree feedback increases team ability to contribute to the organization's goals.

9. 360-degree feedback helps everyone work towards a common standard and institutionalize performance management.

10. In order to improve interpersonal relationships and group cohesiveness, 360-degree feedback is necessary.

11. It promotes self-directed learning and provides a road map for employees' development planning.

12. It promotes better communication within departments.

13. 360-degree feedback Increases the team's ability to contribute to the organization's goals to develop a better bottom line through boosting the organization's capability to meet its objectives.

6.5 Balance Scorecard

The Balance Scorecard (BSC) creates a template for measuring organizational performance as well as individual performance. It is a measurement-based management system, which enables organizations to clarify vision and strategy before initiating action. It is also a monitoring system that integrates strategy into performance measures and targets, making it operational and highly effective. It helps cascade corporate level measures to lower level so that the employees can see what they must do well to improve organizational effectiveness and helps focus the entire organization on what must be done to create breakthrough performance. BSC was introduced in 1992 by Dr. Robert Kaplan and David Nortan and has been successfully adopted by numerous companies worldwide.

Balanced Scorecards are strategic approaches and performance management systems that help organizations implement their visions and strategies. The Balanced Scorecard is a conceptual framework for translating an organization's vision into a set of performance indicators distributed among four perspectives: Financial, Customer, Internal Business Processes, and Learning and Growth. Indicators measure an organization's progress toward achieving its vision. Other indicators are maintained to measure long-term success drivers. Through this scorecard, an organization monitors both its current performance (finance, customer satisfaction, and business process results) and its efforts to improve processes, motivate and educate employees, and enhance information systems – its ability to learn and improve. A Balanced Scorecard enables us to evaluate not just how we have been doing, but also how well we are doing ("current indicators") and can expect to do in the future (leading indicators). This in turn, gives us a clear picture of reality.

The Balanced Scorecard is a way of:

1. Measuring organizational, business unit's or department's success

2. Balancing long-term and short-term actions

3. Balancing different success measures

(a) Financial

(b) The Customer

(c) Internal Operations

(d) Human Resource Systems & Development (learning and growth).

Four Kinds of Balanced Scorecard Measures

The scorecard measures a business from the following perspectives:

1. Financial perspective: Measures reflecting financial performance, such as number of debtors, cash flow or return on investment. Financial performance of an organization is fundamental to its success. Even non-profit organisations must maintain financial stability.

2. Customer perspective: This perspective captures the organization's ability to provide quality goods and services, effective delivery, and overall customer satisfaction for both internal and external customers.

Example: Time taken to process a phone call, customer surveys, complaints or competitive rankings.

3. Business Process perspective: This perspective provides data regarding internal business results against measures that lead to financial success and satisfied customers. To meet organizational objectives and customers' expectations, organizations must identify the key business processes they must excel at. Key processes are monitored to ensure satisfactory outcomes. Internal business processes are the mechanisms through which performance expectations are achieved.

Example: The time spent prospecting new customers, units that required rework or process cost.

4. Learning and growth perspective: This perspective captures the ability of employees, information systems, and organizational alignment to manage the business and adapt to change. Processes will only succeed if adequately skilled and motivated employees, supplied with accurate and timely information, drive them. In order to meet changing requirements and customer expectations, employees are asked to take on dramatically expanded responsibilities. This may require skills, capabilities, technologies, and organizational designs not available before. It measures the company's learning curve for example, the number of employee suggestions or total hours spent on staff training.

Objectives, Measures, Targets and Initiatives of Balance Scorecard

The Balanced Scorecard is a strategic management tool that helps organizations align their activities with their vision and strategy. It consists of four perspectives: financial, customer, internal processes, and learning and growth. For each perspective, the organization should define objectives, measures, targets, and initiatives.

- Objectives: Objectives are the specific goals that the organization wants to achieve in each perspective. These goals should be aligned with the overall vision and strategy of the organization. Examples of objectives could include increasing revenue, improving customer satisfaction, streamlining internal processes, and developing employee skills and capabilities.

- Measures: Measures are the metrics that are used to track progress towards the objectives. These metrics should be specific, measurable, and relevant to the objective. For example, a measure for the objective of increasing revenue could be monthly sales growth, while a measure for the objective of improving customer satisfaction could be the percentage of customers who rate their experience as "excellent" or "very good."

- Targets: Targets are the specific levels of performance that the organization wants to achieve for each measure. Targets should be challenging but achievable, and they should be set based on historical data and industry benchmarks. For example, a target for the monthly sales growth measure could be 10%, while a target for the customer satisfaction measure could be 90%.
- Initiatives: Initiatives are the specific actions that the organization will take to achieve its objectives and targets. These actions should be aligned with the overall strategy of the organization and should be designed to address any gaps or weaknesses in the current performance. For example, an initiative to increase revenue could be to launch a new product line, while an initiative to improve customer satisfaction could be to improve the speed and quality of customer service.

By defining clear objectives, measures, targets, and initiatives for each perspective of the Balanced Scorecard, organizations can align their activities with their strategy, monitor their progress towards their goals, and continuously improve their performance.

Within each of the balanced scorecards financial customer, internal process, and learning perspectives, the organisation must define the following:

1. Strategic objectives – the strategy for achieving that perspective
2. Measures – how progress towards that particular objective will be measured
3. Targets – the target value sought for each measure
4. Initiatives - what will be done to reach the target.

Note: How can Balance Scorecards enhance performance?

The Balanced Scorecard is a strategic management tool used by organizations to align their activities with their vision and strategy. It provides a framework for measuring and managing performance across four key perspectives: financial, customer, internal processes, and learning and growth.

Here are some ways that an organization can enhance performance through the Balanced Scorecard:

- Set Clear Objectives: The first step in using the Balanced Scorecard to enhance performance is to set clear objectives for each of the four perspectives. These objectives should be aligned with the organization's vision and strategy and should be specific, measurable, achievable, relevant, and time-bound (SMART).

- Align Activities: Once the objectives are set, the organization should align its activities with the objectives. This involves ensuring that each department or function within the organization is working towards the same goals and is focused on the right activities to achieve those goals.
- Monitor Progress: The Balanced Scorecard provides a framework for monitoring progress towards the objectives. The organization should regularly track and report on its performance across the four perspectives, using key performance indicators (KPIs) that are linked to the objectives.
- Identify Areas for Improvement: As the organization monitors its performance, it will identify areas where it is not meeting its objectives. These areas should be analyzed to identify the root cause of the problem and to develop a plan for improvement.
- Continuous Learning and Improvement: Finally, the organization should be committed to continuous learning and improvement. This involves using the data collected through the Balanced Scorecard to identify best practices and areas for innovation, and to continuously refine and improve its processes and activities.

By using the Balanced Scorecard to align activities with objectives, monitor progress, identify areas for improvement, and continuously learn and improve, organizations can enhance their performance and achieve their strategic objectives.

The balanced scorecard provides an interconnected model for measuring performance and revolves around four distinct perspectives – financial, customer, internal processes, and innovation and learning. Each of these perspectives is stated in terms of the organisation's objectives, performance measures, targets, and initiatives. All are harnessed to implement corporate vision and strategy.

The name also reflects the balance between short and long-term objectives, between financial and non-financial measures, between lagging and leading indicators and between external and internal performance perspectives.

Under the balance scorecard system, financial measures are the outcome, but do not give an accurate indication of what is or will be occurring on in the organization. Measures of customer satisfaction, growth and retention are the current indicator of company performance. Internal operations (efficiency, speed, reducing non-value-added work, minimizing quality problems) and human resource systems and development are leading indicators of company performance.

Robert S Kaplan and David P Norton, the architects of the balanced scorecard approach, recognized early that long-term improvement in overall performance was unlikely to happen through technology only and hence placed an increasing emphasis on organizational learning and growth. These, in turn, consist of the integrated development of employees', information, and systems capabilities.

6.6 Assessment Centre

An assessment centre is a comprehensive, standardized procedure in which multiple assessment techniques such as situational exercises and job simulations (business games, discussions, reports and presentations) are used to evaluate individual employees for a variety of decisions. Most frequently the approach has been applied to individuals being considered for selection, promotion, placement or special training and development in management.

Promotion

A decision to promote is essentially a decision to select from within the organization those most likely to succeed in higher level jobs. Any method used by the organization to take promotion decisions such as performance appraisal data, interviews, etc. Should be supplemented by assessment centre data. Since the assessment centre method is employed to study the likely performance and behaviour of a person in a role not previously performed by him/her, it can be utilized to supplement promotion decisions. Using additional inputs not only results in a more appropriate decision, but it also eliminates individual biases. It also imparts more transparency and fairness to the promotion system. High validity has been reported in assessment centre data for promotions to first level supervisory and middle management levels; while no validity studies have been reported for higher levels of management.

Tools used in Assessment Centres

As mentioned above, assessment centres have multiple assessment methods using multiple assessors.

The main assessment tools are: **Psychometric Tests**

Assessment centres use three types of tests or questionnaires: aptitude tests, ability tests and personality tests. Aptitude tests attempt to evaluate verbal and numerical reasoning ability. Ability tests measure awareness. Knowledge and other aspects. They also measure simple skills like problem solving ability, etc. For example, a chapter pencil test could be administered to find out the familiarity or level of skill of the individual in relation to computer literacy, financial management skills, etc. Personality tests are those tests aimed at studying various dimensions of personality rather than ability. MBTI and 16PF are tests used in many organizations. There are no right or wrong answers to ability or aptitude tests, but there are no right or wrong answers to personality tests.

The tests are selected for assessment considering the following points:

1. Objective—what needs to be measured;

2. Reliability and validity;

3. Length of time required to administer the test;

4. Availability of qualified experts to administer, scope and interpret the tests;

5. Costs involved.

Assessment centers are a common method used by organizations to evaluate candidates for employment or to assess the development needs of current employees. They typically involve a combination of various assessment tools to evaluate candidates' skills, abilities, and potential for success in a particular role. Here are some of the most common tools used in assessment centers:

a) Role-plays: Role-plays are simulations of workplace situations that require candidates to demonstrate specific skills and abilities, such as communication, problem-solving, and decision-making.

b) In-basket exercises: In-basket exercises require candidates to prioritize and respond to a set of work-related tasks, such as emails, memos, and reports, within a specific time frame.

c) Aptitude and ability tests: Aptitude and ability tests are standardized tests that measure cognitive abilities, such as verbal reasoning, numerical reasoning, and spatial awareness.

d) Personality tests: Personality tests measure an individual's personality traits, such as extraversion, agreeableness, conscientiousness, openness, and emotional stability.

e) Situational judgment tests: Situational judgment tests require candidates to respond to hypothetical workplace scenarios and evaluate different courses of action based on their potential outcomes.

f) Group exercises: Group exercises involve candidates working together on a task or project to evaluate their communication, teamwork, and leadership skills.

g) Interviews: Interviews are a common assessment tool used to evaluate candidates' fit for the role and to gain additional insight into their skills, experience, and personality.

h) Psychometric assessments: Psychometric assessments are tests that measure a range of cognitive, behavioural, and emotional characteristics, such as aptitude, personality, and emotional intelligence.

i) Presentation exercises: Presentation exercises require candidates to prepare and deliver a presentation on a given topic to assess their communication and presentation skills.

j) Case studies: Case studies require candidates to analyze and solve a complex problem or scenario to evaluate their critical thinking, problem-solving, and decision-making skills.

In general, the selection of assessment tools used in an assessment center will depend on the specific needs of the organization and the role being evaluated. A combination of multiple assessment tools is often used to provide a comprehensive evaluation of candidates' skills and abilities.

Task: Which of the following appraisal methods is most appropriate for evaluating the following types of employees?

1. IT professionals

2. HR professional

3. Research professionals

Give a suitable example of how you would choose a particular method

6.7 Common Rating Errors

Differences in perception and value systems influence evaluations. For instance, two appraisers observe an employee disagreeing with a supervisor. One perceives this as insubordination, but the other sees it as a willingness to stand up for what he believes in. As a result of individual bias, appraisal credibility can seriously compromise appraisal credibility. Some common syndromes are:

1. Halo Effect: This is a tendency to let the assessment of a single trait influence the evaluation of the individual on other traits too.

2. Horns Effect: There is a tendency for one negative trait of an individual to colour the entire appraisal of an employee as a result of the Horns Effect. This results in a lower rating than warranted.

3. Leniency or Constant Error: Depending upon the appraiser's own value system which acts as a standard, employees may be rated leniently or strictly. Such a rating does not refer to the actual performance of employees. Some appraisers consistently assign high values to all employees, regardless of merit. This is a leniency error. The strictness tendency is a reverse situation, where all individuals are rated too severely and their performance is understated.

4. Central Tendency: This is the most common error that occurs when a rather assigns most middle range scores or values to all individuals under appraisal. Extremely high or extremely low evaluations are avoided by assigning 'average ratings' to all.

5. Spill-over Effect: This refers to allowing past performance to influence the evaluation of present performance.

6. Personal Bias: Perhaps the most significant error of all arises from the fact that very few people are capable of making objective judgments entirely independent of their values and prejudices.

The above errors have raised concerns about performance appraisal. According to McGregor (1960), appraisal is a judgmental process that demotivates employees. Similar concerns were voiced by Deming (1982) who suggested that appraisal was 'a deadly disease' which blamed individuals for systematic problems within organizations. Margerison (1976) predicted appraisal would 'fall apart at the seams' due to managerial indifference, employee ambivalence and union opposition. This theme was reiterated by Fletcher (1993), who suggested that standardized appraisal days were numbered. But, despite these gloomy predictions, performance appraisal has flourished.

Case Study: Competency-based Balanced Scorecard Model: An Integrative Perspective

In the current globalization induced by abrupt changes in business environment, human resources have become the source of successful corporate strategy. This study emphasizes that human resource and HR practices are the foundation for achieving business excellence in terms of ROI, market share, employee satisfaction and customer delight. The paper explains the implementation of Balanced Scorecard by developing competencies in relation to values of the organization necessary for achieving business excellence."

Introduction

In today's dynamic world, companies are adopting newer approaches for facing competition and achieving business excellence. The new economic paradigm is characterized by speed, innovation, quality and customer satisfaction. The essence of the competitive advantage has shifted from tangible assets to intangible ones. Earlier, HR was concerned with activities such as payroll, staffing and employee welfare but rules of game have started to change completely as today organizations have to reckon with global competition and match international requirements in terms of product design, process technology, quality standards and on time delivery.

It is said today that business endeavours succeed or fail because of the people involved. Only by attracting the most talented people and making them perform well will we be able to accomplish our deeds. Based on various studies (Pfeffer & Jeffrey 1994) it can be concluded that firms with more effective HR management systems consistently outperform the competition. However, evidence that HR can contribute to a firm's success doesn't mean it is now effectively contributing to the success of the firm. Managers struggle to make HR a strategic asset. This case demonstrates that human resource and business success are connected in terms of tangible and intangible measures. It establishes a framework to help HR professionals make human resources a strategic asset.

Based on Balanced Scorecard (Kaplan & Norton 1996) and through competency framework evident from corporate practices, the author has established a Competency-based Balanced Scorecard Model.

Balanced Scorecard

Developed in the early 1990s by Kaplan and Norton (1992), the Balanced Scorecard is a management system that enables organizations to clarify their vision and strategy and translate them into action and has become a prominent strategic tool for the management.

6.8 Summary

• Structure and Sayles classify performance appraisal into three groups: traditional performance rating, new-rating methods and result-oriented appraisal.

• Frequently called 'multi-rater feedback', 360-degree feedback is a comprehensive appraisal in which employee feedback is received from all sources that interact specifically with the employee on a daily basis.

• Appraisers are more crucial than appraisal methods. It is desirable to make the immediate superior an integral part of the appraisal program.

• Performance is a thing of the past, while potential includes the possible knowledge, skills and attitudes the employee may possess for better performance.

6.9 Keywords

• 360-degree Feedback or Appraisal: It is the most comprehensive appraisal where feedback about the employees' performance comes from all the sources that come into contact with the employee on his job.

• The Balance Scorecard: It creates a template for measuring organizational and individual performance and enables organizations to clarify vision and strategy before initiating action.

• Traditional Rating: It involves the immediate supervisor of the individual being evaluated.

6.10 Self-Assessment

Fill in the blanks:

1. In .... method of appraisal, the immediate superior to the employee fills up a performance review form.

2. In .... method, the employees are assessed relatively to the other employees working in his group.

3. Internal customers are also known as .... whose feedback on employee performance improves team spirit.

4. An employee's current evaluation is largely influenced by his previous performance. This type of error is known as ....

5. Performance appraisal is present-oriented, whereas .... appraisal is future oriented.

State whether the following statements are true or false:

6. Performance appraisals can be formal or informal.

7. MBO may be viewed as a management system rather than an appraisal method.

8. 360-degree appraisals are generally considered less appropriate for managers.

9. Traditional rating involves the immediate supervisor of the evaluated individual.

10. 360-degree feedback is a time-consuming and expensive assessment process.

Answers: Self-Assessment

1. traditional rating 2. forced distribution

3. Peers 4. spill over effect

5. potential appraisal 6. True

7. True 8. False
9. True 10. True

6.11 Review Questions

1. Analyze the traditional rating method and the current rating method of appraisal.

2. "MBO is a tool that is inextricably connected with team building so that team members' work commitment can be increased and their desire to excel in performance can be inspired." Discuss.

3. How 360-degree feedback system adds value to an organization?

4. "Performance appraisal is plagued by rating errors." Describe the statement.

5. How does the newer rating method differ from the traditional method for rating performance?

6. Why 360-degree feedback is also known as 'multi-ratter feedback'?

7. How will you minimize common rating errors on performance appraisals?

8. Discuss 360-degree appraisal scope.

9. Which performance appraisal method is best for HR professionals?

10. "Goals should be set by manager-subordinate pairs, and also by teams." Discuss.

CHAPTER SEVEN

Performance Monitoring

Objectives

After studying this unit, you can:
- Describe the traits and goals of performance monitoring.
- Describe the purpose and methodology of performance monitoring.

Introduction

Performance management is a continuous process of managing and developing performance standards, which reflect normal good practices of setting direction, monitoring and measuring performance, providing feedback, and taking action. This concept bears frequent repetition, and is one of the most important concepts in performance management. Managers shouldn't be forced to perform performance management as something 'special'. It should also not be imposed as something 'special' on individuals or teams. As a framework, performance management helps managers and their teams understand what must be accomplished, how it can be achieved, and how to improve.

Performance monitoring is the process of gathering and analyzing data about the behavior and efficiency of a system, application, or network. The purpose of performance monitoring is to identify and resolve issues that may negatively impact the performance and availability of the system, application, or network.

Performance monitoring involves collecting and analyzing data on various metrics such as response time, throughput, error rates, CPU usage, memory usage, and network latency. This data can be used to identify bottlenecks, track trends, and make informed decisions about capacity planning and resource allocation.

Performance monitoring can be performed at different levels of the technology stack, from the hardware and operating system level, to the application and network level. Monitoring can be done using various tools and techniques, such as log analysis, real-time monitoring, and synthetic monitoring.

In summary, performance monitoring is a critical process that helps ensure that systems, applications, and networks are running smoothly and efficiently, and that any issues are detected and resolved before they cause significant problems.

Note: The monitoring of manager performance follows naturally from the planning of manager performance in supervisory leadership. It is during this phase that the cycle of

PfM: Planning $\rightarrow$ Monitoring $\rightarrow$ Stocking occurs several times.

7.1 Performance Monitoring: Concept and Characteristics

Performance monitoring involves assessing an environment of continuous learning and development, maintaining employee performance, and developing individual competencies to increase productivity for an organization. For business management to be successful, performance must be monitored continuously to generate data that can be used to determine whether particular strategies have been successful. Management must be informed about current performance in order to realistically improve performance. Key performance indicators (KPIs) should be identified to enable management to monitor progress in this regard.

American Compensation Association (1996) states that open, honest, positive, two-way communication is essential for performance management. Individuals and teams receive instant feedback on their performance based on what they have done well and what they have done wrong. Providing people with the information they need to monitor their own performance is ideal, it is not available readily, they can be encouraged to seek it. People are motivated by autonomy and the ability to control their work when given autonomy.

Monthly, quarterly, etc., interim informal evaluations might be conducted. As circumstances change, objectives and plans can be revised to reflect current conditions, providing more structured feedback.

The given below are the key characteristics of performance monitoring:

1. Data collection can be managed and documented with the help of a performance monitoring plan.

2. A performance management system must include performance monitoring.

3. The purpose of performance monitoring is to maintain the employees'

performance according to the organization's goals and objectives.

4. Management and employees can build strong relationships through performance monitoring.

5. It makes it easier for workers to advance in their careers.

6. Performance monitoring gives employees the opportunity to take training and develop their skills.

Note:

Some Managerial Behaviours in Monitoring and Mentoring are represented here:

1. An appreciation of good performance.

2. Identifying a fault in a person's behaviour without rejecting them.

3. It is better to share feelings rather than make value judgments.

4. Integrity in behaviour and intent must be demonstrated and demanded.

5. Easily accessible to fulfil legitimate needs of her managers.

6. Reaffirming the importance of effective managers to the organization continuously.

Performance monitoring is the ongoing process of measuring, analyzing, and optimizing the performance of a system, application, or network. This includes tracking various metrics and identifying potential bottlenecks or areas for improvement. Here are some of the key concepts and characteristics of performance monitoring:

- Metrics: Performance monitoring involves tracking various metrics related to the system, application, or network being monitored. These metrics can include response time, throughput, error rates, CPU usage, memory usage, and network latency.

- Real-time monitoring: Real-time monitoring involves monitoring systems, applications, and networks in real-time. This allows for the detection of issues as soon as they occur, enabling quick response and resolution.

- Historical data analysis: Historical data analysis involves analyzing past performance data to identify trends and patterns. This can help identify potential issues before they occur and inform future capacity planning and resource allocation decisions.

- Alerting and notifications: Performance monitoring tools often include alerting and notification features, which can be configured to notify system administrators or other relevant parties when certain thresholds are exceeded or issues are detected.

- Resource utilization analysis: Performance monitoring can help identify areas of resource utilization that can be optimized, such as CPU usage, memory usage, or disk I/O. This can help improve overall system performance and reduce costs.
- End-user experience monitoring: Performance monitoring can also include monitoring the end-user experience, such as website load times or application responsiveness. This can help ensure a positive user experience and prevent user frustration.

Overall, performance monitoring is an essential aspect of maintaining the health and performance of systems, applications, and networks. By tracking and analyzing key metrics, identifying potential issues, and optimizing resource utilization, performance monitoring can help ensure that systems and applications run efficiently and provide a positive user experience.

7.2 Objectives of Performance Monitoring

During performance planning or expectation setting and subsequent review meetings, PfM explicitly promotes the importance of the manager and her manager taking joint responsibility for monitoring progress towards goals and tasks. Managers use tools such as written reports, reviews, and inspections to monitor:

1. Management tasks and goals are completed on time and in a quality manner.

2. Management assistance and support that is legitimately needed by the managee's tasks, including those agreed upon during meetings and review sessions.

3. Measurement methods and techniques should be improved in order to improve employee performance.

4. The process of continuous learning and development is introduced.

Periodic Reviews: How Do They Work Better and Help?

Performance managers benefit from periodic reviews in the following ways:

1. Before it's too late, correct planning assumptions and errors midway.

2. Ensure progress is being monitored and encouraged, and keep the project on track.

3. Ensure a strong dyadic relationship between the manager and her employee.

The primary objectives of performance monitoring are to ensure that systems, applications, and networks are running smoothly and efficiently, and that any issues are detected and resolved before they cause significant problems. Here are some specific objectives of performance monitoring:

• Identify and troubleshoot performance issues: Performance monitoring is used to detect performance issues and identify their root causes. This helps system administrators and developers troubleshoot and resolve problems quickly.

• Optimize system performance: Performance monitoring provides insight into system resource utilization, such as CPU and memory usage. This information can be used to optimize system performance by identifying and addressing bottlenecks or underutilized resources.

• Predict and prevent problems: By tracking historical data and trends, performance monitoring can be used to predict potential performance issues and prevent them from occurring. This helps ensure system availability and reliability.

• Monitor service level agreements (SLAs): Performance monitoring can be used to monitor compliance with SLAs, such as response time requirements. This helps ensure that the system or application is meeting its service level commitments.

• Support capacity planning: Performance monitoring provides insight into resource utilization and capacity requirements. This information can be used to support capacity planning efforts and ensure that the system or application has the resources it needs to meet demand.

• Improve user experience: Performance monitoring can help ensure that users have a positive experience with the system or application by identifying and addressing performance issues that may impact user satisfaction.

Generally, the objectives of performance monitoring are to ensure system availability and reliability, optimize system performance, and improve the user experience. By achieving these objectives, organizations can improve efficiency, reduce costs, and provide better service to their users.

7.3 Importance of Performance Monitoring

Performance monitoring is critical for ensuring the health and reliability of systems, applications, and networks. Here are some key reasons why performance monitoring is important:

• Early detection of issues: Performance monitoring enables the early detection of issues before they become critical problems. This allows system administrators to take action to resolve issues before they have a significant impact on users or the business.

• Faster troubleshooting and resolution: Performance monitoring provides visibility into the performance of systems, applications, and networks. This enables system administrators to quickly troubleshoot and resolve issues, reducing downtime and minimizing the impact on users.

• Improved user experience: Performance monitoring can help improve the user experience by ensuring that systems and applications are running smoothly and efficiently. This can reduce frustration and improve user satisfaction.

• Cost savings: Performance monitoring can help optimize system performance and resource utilization. By identifying and addressing bottlenecks and underutilized resources, organizations can reduce costs and maximize the value of their investments.

• Compliance and service level agreement (SLA) monitoring: Performance monitoring can help organizations monitor compliance with SLAs and ensure that systems and applications are meeting service level commitments. This is important for maintaining customer satisfaction and avoiding penalties for non-compliance.

• Capacity planning: Performance monitoring can provide insight into resource utilization and capacity requirements. This information can be used to support capacity planning efforts and ensure that the system or application has the resources it needs to meet demand.

In summary, performance monitoring is important for early issue detection, faster troubleshooting and resolution, improved user experience, cost savings, compliance and SLA monitoring, and capacity planning. By implementing effective performance monitoring strategies, organizations can improve the reliability and efficiency of their systems, applications, and networks.

Monitoring performance is crucial for the following reasons:
1. As a result of performance monitoring, the existing performance management system can be modified, changed, or altered.
2. As a result of the organization's mission and objectives, it helps to review and correct performance objectives.
3. A competency improvement plan identifies areas for improvement.
4. Employees perform better as a result of it.

5. The ability to realize the full potential of employees and the organization for excellence in performance is improved.

7.4 Process of Performance Monitoring

The process of performance monitoring involves several key steps that help ensure that systems, applications, and networks are running smoothly and efficiently. Here are the main steps involved in the process of performance monitoring:

- Define metrics: The first step in performance monitoring is to identify the metrics that need to be monitored. These metrics can include response time, throughput, error rates, CPU usage, memory usage, and network latency.
- Select monitoring tools: Once the metrics have been identified, the next step is to select the appropriate monitoring tools. There are a variety of tools available, ranging from log analysis to real-time monitoring to synthetic monitoring.
- Configure monitoring: The monitoring tools must be configured to collect data on the identified metrics. This can involve setting thresholds for alerts and notifications, defining data collection intervals, and configuring dashboards and reports.
- Collect and analyze data: Once the monitoring tools are configured, they will begin collecting data on the identified metrics. This data is analyzed to identify performance issues, bottlenecks, and trends.
- Alert and notify: The monitoring tools are configured to send alerts and notifications when certain thresholds are exceeded or issues are detected. This allows system administrators to quickly respond to issues and take appropriate action.
- Troubleshoot and optimize: When issues are detected, system administrators must troubleshoot and identify the root cause of the problem. This may involve adjusting resource allocation, optimizing code or configuration, or upgrading hardware.
- Evaluate and adjust: Finally, the performance monitoring process is evaluated and adjusted based on the results achieved. This may involve refining the metrics being monitored, adjusting thresholds, or selecting different monitoring tools.

Overall, the process of performance monitoring is an ongoing and iterative process that involves identifying metrics, selecting monitoring tools, configuring monitoring, collecting and analyzing data, alerting and notifying, troubleshooting and optimizing, and evaluating and adjusting. By following this process, organizations can ensure that their systems, applications, and networks are running smoothly and efficiently.

Note:

Managers observe manager performance in the following ways:

1. Reports written on a regular basis

2. Arrangements for meetings

3. An on-the-spot inspection, or a field trip or site visit if a manager's location does not coincide with that of their subordinates.

4. The information provided by other sources should be relevant and reliable.

Note:

Management involves providing feedback to managers and asking managers for feedback during monitoring

1. Meetings with groups or teams to discuss common issues and problems.

2. The meeting aims to address specific issues and problems encountered by the manage(s).

As a result, the manager and the manage discuss corrective measures that will be taken, actions to be taken by either or both, and additional help needed to complete the tasks and accomplish the goals.

Task: Discuss the performance monitoring system at ICICI Bank.

7.5 Summary

• The performance monitoring process provides opportunities for modifying, changing and/or altering the existing performance management system.

• Monitoring performance is the process of assessing the environment of continuous learning and development, maintaining the employee's performance, and developing individual competencies to increase employee productivity.

• For successful business management, it is imperative to continuously monitor performance in order to generate data by which to judge specific strategies' success or failure.

• It is also possible to monitor progress in implementing the personal development plan throughout the year.

• Data collection can be managed, documented, and planned with a performance monitoring plan.

• Traditional organizational expectations and more contemporary methods are bridged through coaching and mentoring.

7.6 Keywords

Performance monitoring: The process of performance monitoring involves evaluating the organization's learning environment, maintaining the employee's performance, and developing individual competencies to better serve the organization.

KPI: Key Performance Indicators.

7.7 Self-Assessment

Fill in the blanks:

1. Successful business management requires the .... of performance to generate data by which to judge the success or otherwise of specific strategies.

2. Progress in implementing the .... can also be monitored during the year.

3. .... explicitly promotes the value that a manager and her supervisor accept joint responsibility for monitoring progress on the tasks and goals agreed upon during the initial performance planning or expectation setting meeting and subsequent review meetings.

4. Improvement in performance can only be realistically achieved when management is properly informed about ....

5. Performance monitoring identifies areas for .... improvement.

6. Progress in implementing the .... can also be monitored during the year.

7. Performance monitoring helps in maintaining the employees' performance as per the............................ of the organisation.

State whether the following statements are true or false:

8. Training and development are not internal parts of performance monitoring.

9. Performance monitoring provides scope for modification.

10. Monitoring facilitates employees' career development.

Answers: Self-Assessment

1. ongoing monitoring 2. personal development plan

3. PfM 4. current performance

5. competency 6. personal development plan

7. goals and objectives 8. False

9. True 10. True

7.8 Review Questions

1. The American Compensation Association (1996) states that it is a necessity to develop performance management on the basis of 'open, honest, positive, two-way communication between supervisors and employees throughout the period'. Discuss.

2. Design a standard monitoring process for the banking industry.

3. Explain how performance monitoring contributes to the success of performance management systems.

4. Why should managers provide ongoing feedback to employees about their performance?

5. Why is feedback a critical component of performance monitoring?

6. "Performance monitoring plays a vital role in achieving organizations goals and objectives." How?

7. How will you identify a manager's monitoring and mentoring behaviour?

8. When it comes to building a strong relationship between management and an employee, how does performance monitoring help?

9. Discuss the importance of performance monitoring in achieving organizational objectives.

10. "Performance management should not be imposed on managers as something 'special' they have to do." Discuss.

Further Readings

• Books Aubrey C. Daniels, Bringing out the Best in People, 2nd edition, McGraw-Hill, 1999.

• BD Singh, Performance Management Systems, Excel Books, New Delhi.

• Business Performance Management, Magazine, Matt Weiner.

• Cynthia D Fisher, Human Resource Management, 5th Edition-Biztantra.

• Dixit Varsha, Performance Management, 1st edition, Vrinda Publications Ltd.

• Herman Aguinis, Performance Management, Pearson Education, 2007.

• Kevin R Murphy, Understanding Performance Appraisal: Social, Jeanette Cleveland.

• Routledge Taylor and Francis Group, Journal of Organizational Behavior Management, Published Quarterly, 2009.

• Tapomoy Deb, Performance Appraisal and Management, Excel Books, New Delhi.

• Thomas C. Mawhinney, William K. Redmon and Carl Merle Johnson, Handbook of Organizational Performance, Routledge. 2001